BASIC MANDARIN CHINESE

READING & WRITING

PRACTICE BOOK

CORNELIUS C. KUBLER & JERLING GUO KUBLER

TUTTLE Publishing

Tokyo | Rutland, Vermont | Singapore

Published by Tuttle Publishing, an imprint of Periplus Editions (HK) Ltd.

www.tuttlepublishing.com

ISBN 978-0-8048-4727-8
(Previously published under ISBN 978-0-8048-4017-0)

Distributed by

North America, Latin America & Europe
Tuttle Publishing
364 Innovation Drive, North Clarendon,
VT 05759-9436 U.S.A.
Tel: 1 (802) 773-8930; Fax: 1 (802) 773-6993
info@tuttlepublishing.com
www.tuttlepublishing.com

Japan
Tuttle Publishing
Yaekari Building, 3rd Floor 5-4-12 Osaki
Shinagawa-ku, Tokyo 141 0032
Tel: (81) 3 5437-0171; Fax: (81) 3 5437-0755
sales@tuttle.co.jp
www.tuttle.co.jp

Asia Pacific
Berkeley Books Pte. Ltd.
3 Kallang Sector #04-01, Singapore 349278
Tel: (65) 6741-2178; Fax: (65) 6741-2179
inquiries@periplus.com.sg
www.tuttlepublishing.com

23 22 21 20 10 9 8 7 6 5 4 3

Printed in Malaysia 2011VP

The Bonus Material from the enclosed CD-ROM may also be Downloaded.

How to Download the Bonus Material of this Book.

1. You must have an internet connection.
2. Type the URL below into your web browser.

http://www.tuttlepublishing.com/basic-mandarin-chinese-reading-writing-practice-book-downloadable-cd-content

For support email us at info@tuttlepublishing.com.

A Note to the Learner

When it comes to learning Chinese, practice is essential, of course. This workbook offers you many options for practicing and polishing your written Chinese, and was designed to be used in conjunction with the textbook *Basic Mandarin Chinese Reading & Writing* as well as its companion volumes *Basic Mandarin Chinese Speaking & Listening* and *Basic Mandarin Chinese Speaking & Listening Practice Book*. However, this workbook may be used to hone reading and writing skills no matter which textbook or course you're using to learn Chinese.

These are some of the special features of *Basic Mandarin Chinese Reading & Writing Practice Book*:

- This workbook has been designed so it can be used either **in a class** with an instructor or by **independent learners** working on their own.
- Both **simplified and traditional characters** are taught and practiced in the same volume. This means students can learn either or both kinds of characters without having to purchase another book; and instructors have the flexibility to teach a combined class where some students read and write one type of characters and other students the other type.
- This workbook provides **character practice sheets** for the 288 characters introduced in *Basic Mandarin Chinese Reading & Writing*, with complete information on stroke order and direction for both the simplified and traditional forms of the characters.
- A wide variety of **reading and writing exercises** is included, such as dictation, fill-in-the-blank, dialog completion, answering questions, map reading, converting written style to spoken style, identifying radicals and phonetics, and punctuating sentences.
- Exercises are included that involve **written tasks based on realia** such as schedules, tables, calendars, photographs, and name cards.
- English-Chinese **translation exercises** are provided for each unit.
- There are **printable flash cards** for all the new characters and words, with Chinese characters on one side and Pinyin and English on the other.
- **Electronic flash cards** are also available at a special website.
- An **included disc** offers native-speaker audio for dictation practice.
- The *Basic Mandarin Chinese* **Instructor's Guide** (available free from the publisher) contains detailed suggestions for using these materials as well as a wealth of exercises for use by instructors in class or by tutors during practice sessions.

附注

《基础中文：读与写》练习册专供读写课使用，提供大量的阅读与写作练习，极为实用。学习者宜与配套的《基础中文：读与写》、《基础中文：听与说》及《基础中文：听与说》练习册一起使用。本练习册亦可作为任何初级中文课程之补充教材，以提高学习者的读写能力。此套教材包括一张光盘的《基础中文教师手册》，指导教师如何使用此教材。

附注

《基礎中文：讀與寫》練習冊專供讀寫課使用，提供大量的閱讀與寫作練習，極為實用。學習者宜與配套的《基礎中文：讀與寫》、《基礎中文：聽與說》及《基礎中文：聽與說》練習冊一起使用。本練習冊亦可作為任何初級中文課程之補充教材，以提高學習者的讀寫能力。此套教材包括一張光盤的《基礎中文教師手冊》，指導教師如何使用此教材。

Acknowledgments

I'm indebted to a number of people for their assistance in the preparation of this volume. It's not possible to mention everyone who participated, but special thanks are due the following for their contributions:

For writing the simplified and traditional characters on the character practice sheets: Su-Ling Huang, Yun-O Huang-Li, Minjun Jiang, Jerling Guo Kubler, Ching-yi Sun, and Zhe Zhang. Youlin Shi and Xiaohong Wan also assisted in selecting characters for revision.

For assistance in drafting the map exercises: Hoyoon Nam.

For assistance in drafting the paper flash cards: Nikki Fang.

For creating the electronic flash cards: Daniel Nelson.

For allowing themselves to be photographed: Kevin DeWar, Boji Lam, Zachary Whitney, and Dongshan Zhang.

For advice and assistance with computer-related work: Adam Jianjun Wang, Senior Instructional Technology specialist at Williams College, and Peter Leimbigler of Asia Communications Québec Inc. All of the Chinese language content in this volume was processed using the KEY 5.1 Chinese language software that Dr. Leimbigler and his colleagues developed.

For meticulous editing and many other helpful suggestions during the production of this course: Sandra Korinchak, former Senior Editor at Tuttle Publishing. I also wish to express my appreciation for their enthusiastic support of the project and its development to Tuttle's Publisher Eric Oey and Vice President Christina Ong; and my heartfelt thanks for their expertise and assistance throughout go to Nancy Goh, Ngo Su Yin, and the entire Tuttle Sales and Marketing team.

Logistical and financial support from Dr. Jenny F. So and staff of the Institute of Chinese Studies at the Chinese University of Hong Kong is gratefully acknowledged. I also wish to express my appreciation to Clement Chu-sing Lau and Celia Lai Ngo Poon for helping make our stay in Hong Kong in spring 2011 so productive and pleasant.

Last but not least, I wish to thank the students in the Basic Chinese classes at Williams College from 1993 through 2010 for their corrections, suggestions, encouragement, and inspiration.

Cornelius C. Kubler
Department of Asian Studies
Williams College
Williamstown, Massachusetts, USA

Contents

A Note to the Learner 3

Acknowledgments 4

How to Use These Materials 6

1. Character Practice Sheets 9

2. Reading and Writing Exercises 105

3. Translation Exercises 201

On Disc 4. **Flash Cards** (288 double-sided cards)

Includes practice materials for these 12 topics:

Unit A: Numbers, Personal Names, and Place Names

Unit B: People, Places, Streets, and Roads

Unit 1: Greetings and Useful Phrases

Unit 2: Introductions

Unit 3: Numbers, Dates, Time, and Money (I)

Unit 4: Numbers, Dates, Time, and Money (II)

Unit 5: Locating Persons, Places, and Things

Unit 6: Biographical Information (I)

Unit 7: Biographical Information (II)

Unit 8: Getting Around Beijing (I)

Unit 9: Getting Around Beijing (II)

Unit 10: Weather

See Disc for Audio!

How to Use These Materials

Basic Mandarin Chinese Reading & Writing Practice Book is the workbook designed to accompany the textbook *Basic Mandarin Chinese Reading & Writing*. It offers you a wide variety of activities for both in- and out-of-class learning, to help you reinforce and "activize" your learning of the new characters, vocabulary, grammar, and related material introduced in the textbook.

The pages of this workbook have been perforated to facilitate their removal for correction by an instructor (or by a tutor or native-speaking friend, in the case of independent learners), and then may be kept in a binder for reference.

Character Practice Sheets

The first section of *Basic Mandarin Chinese Reading & Writing Practice Book* consists of character practice sheets for all the new characters in units A, B, and 1–10 for you to study, fill out, and hand in to your instructor or mentor for correction and comments. A sheet with the six characters for a lesson in simplified form always comes first, followed by a sheet with the same six characters in traditional form on the back side of the page. We recommend that you eventually learn to recognize both types of characters, though it's sufficient if you learn how to write only one type.

Being able to handwrite characters is important not only for writing but also for reading, since if you can write a character correctly from memory, you're more likely to be able to recognize it and distinguish it from other similar characters. Later on in your study of Chinese, you'll also want to learn how to process Chinese characters using computers, but we feel it's important for beginning students to have experience in writing characters by hand.

On the practice sheets, there are two kinds of model characters for your reference. To the left, in the large boxes, are large versions of each character with small Arabic numbers indicating the *order* and *direction* of the strokes. Note that the location of each number indicates where that stroke begins. Then, to the right of the large characters, in the smaller boxes, there is a stroke-by-stroke build-up of each character which further clarifies the stroke order. The purpose of the handwritten characters is not to serve as examples of calligraphy, but rather to instruct learners in accurate and legible handwriting of the characters, as written with pen or pencil by ordinary Chinese writers today.

Be sure to follow the correct stroke order and direction. If you don't, your characters will not only not look right, but you might have difficulty in using dictionaries, since these are traditionally based on the number of strokes in characters or character components. The accuracy of handwriting recognition software might also be affected if strokes are written in the wrong order and direction. And if you're not familiar with correct stroke order, you may in the future have problems reading and writing Chinese cursive script, since which strokes can be connected and which cannot is closely related to the order and direction of the individual strokes.

Beginning with the first empty box after the end of the stroke-by-stroke build-up, you should write the *entire character* in each empty box until all the boxes for that character have been filled. Write slowly and carefully, referring back often to the stroke direction and stroke order of the models. We recommend that you use either number 2 pencil or black or blue pen. As you write each character, say its pronunciation out loud and think of the meaning. You'll probably want to have your textbook open for reference. Many learners find it helpful to write the Pinyin and basic English meaning of each character to the left of the large character on the practice sheets.

Even though there is an agreed upon stroke order for the majority of characters, there exists a small number of characters that have common alternate stroke orders, e.g., 方. For the sake of consistency, in the case of simplified characters we follow the stroke order promulgated by the Working Committee on National Language and Script and published in Beijing by Yuwen Chubanshe as 现代汉语通用字笔顺规范 (5th printing 1999). In the case of traditional characters, we follow the stroke order promulgated by the Committee on the Promotion of Mandarin and published in Taipei by the Ministry of Education as 常用國字標準字筆順手冊 (3rd revised printing 2008).

Reading and Writing Exercises

This book includes two pages of reading and writing exercises for each of the four parts of every unit of *Basic Mandarin Chinese Reading & Writing*. The first section of the reading and writing exercises consists of three phrases or sentences for dictation.* You should listen to the corresponding section of the included disc and transcribe what you hear into Chinese characters. Since this is for practice and not a test, you're encouraged to listen as many times as you wish and, when needed, to consult your textbook or its glossaries.

Beginning with Unit 1, the second section of the reading and writing exercises includes four questions that you should answer in Chinese characters. The first two questions are always based on portions of the corresponding lesson in *Basic Mandarin Chinese Reading & Writing*, to which you should refer as you answer the questions, while the last two questions are addressed to you, the learner, and may be answered any way you wish.

The last section of the reading and writing exercises includes a wide variety of exercises involving scrambled sentences, dialog completion, fill-in-the blank, answering questions, word study, map reading, converting written style to spoken style, distinguishing different usages of characters, punctuating sentences, stroke order, radicals, and phonetics, as well as a number of exercises based on printed realia from mainland China, Taiwan, and Hong Kong.

Translation Exercises

Ten phrases or sentences for translation from English to Chinese have been included for each unit of *Basic Mandarin Chinese Reading & Writing*. The purpose of the translation exercises is to provide you with additional practice in writing the characters, using the grammar patterns, and practicing the important vocabulary of the unit, and to serve as a check of mastery over the material. Completing the translation exercises will be helpful to you in reviewing for the unit tests.

The sentences should be translated into Chinese characters with correct punctuation in the blank space that has been left under each sentence. The English in the translation exercises is in some places purposely somewhat stilted, to guide you toward the correct Chinese translation. In certain cases, additional instructions have been added in parentheses within or after the English sentence, for example, to be polite or to use or not use certain words. If you've forgotten the Chinese equivalent for an English word or grammar pattern, you can consult the various glossaries and indices in the back of *Basic Mandarin Chinese Reading & Writing* and *Basic Mandarin Chinese Speaking & Listening*.

It's recommended that the instructor correct and return the translation exercises to students before the test on the corresponding unit, so that any remaining problems can be identified and addressed in a timely manner. Students should carefully study the instructor's corrections, making sure they understand the reason for any errors, and then file the corrected exercises for later reference.

Flash Cards

Flash cards are an excellent aid in memorization. They work based on the principle of spaced repetition, that is, gradually increasing the interval between each time that you recall information correctly. We recommend that you take along a couple of dozen flash cards from *Basic Mandarin Chinese Reading & Writing Practice Book* wherever you go. Use "empty" time you spend waiting in line, on a bus, or before classes begin to study the flash cards. You can look at the character side and test yourself on the pronunciation and meaning of the characters, or you can look at the English side and try to reconstruct from that the correct pronunciation and characters. Your goal should be to identify those characters and words you still have problems with and remove them from the larger set for special study.

* Scripts for the dictation exercises are included in the *Instructor's Guide*.

Flash cards are available for *Basic Mandarin Chinese Reading & Writing*. This consists of traditional paper flash cards, one card for each of the 288 new characters. The paper flash cards have been designed with Chinese characters (simplified and traditional) on one side, and Pinyin and English on the other side. Both the new characters of each lesson and the individual words written with those characters are included on the flash cards. In the lower left-hand corner on both sides of every card are given the unit and part number, while in the lower right-hand corner is given the number of the character in this course. Due to page limitations and in an effort to control costs, the paper flash cards have been included on the enclosed disc for users to print out themselves as needed. The flash cards should be carefully printed—first all the pages with Chinese characters, then, on the other side, the pages with Pinyin and English, after which each page of eight flash cards can be cut apart with a paper cutter or scissors.

Unit A, Part 1: Character Practice Sheet (Simplified Characters)

NAME ____________________ COURSE ____________________ DATE ____________________

一	一									
二	一	二								
三	一	二	三							
四	丨	冂			四					
五	一	丅		五						
王	一	二	干	王						

Unit A, Part 1: Character Practice Sheet (Traditional Characters)

NAME ______________________ COURSE ______________________ DATE ______________________

一	一									
二	一	二								
三	一	二	三							
四	丨	冂	冂	四	四					
五	一	丅	五	五						
王	一	二	干	王						

Unit A, Part 2: Character Practice Sheet (Simplified Characters)

NAME ______________________ COURSE ______________________ DATE ______________________

六 (1 2 3 4)	丶	亠	亠丿	六				
七 (1 2)	一	七						
八 (1 2)	丿	八						
九 (1 2)	丿	九						
十 (1 2)	一	十						
林 (1 2 3 4 5 6 7 8)	一	十	才	木	木一	村	材	林

Unit A, Part 2: Character Practice Sheet (Traditional Characters)

NAME ____________________ COURSE ____________________ DATE ____________________

六	丶	亠	亠丿	六						
七	一	七								
八	丿	八								
九	丿	九								
十	一	十								
林	一	十	才	木	木一	木十	材	林		

Unit A, Part 3: Character Practice Sheet (Simplified Characters)

NAME ______________________ COURSE ______________________ DATE ______________________

大	一	ナ	大						
山	丨	凵	山						
明	丨	冂	月	日	日丿	日冂	日月	明	
北	丨	十	丬	丬丶	北				
京	丶	亠	亠丨	亠冂	亠口	亠口亅	亠口小	京	
台	𠃋	厶	厶丨	厶𠃍	台				

Unit A, Part 3: Character Practice Sheet (Traditional Characters)

NAME ______________________ COURSE ______________________ DATE ______________________

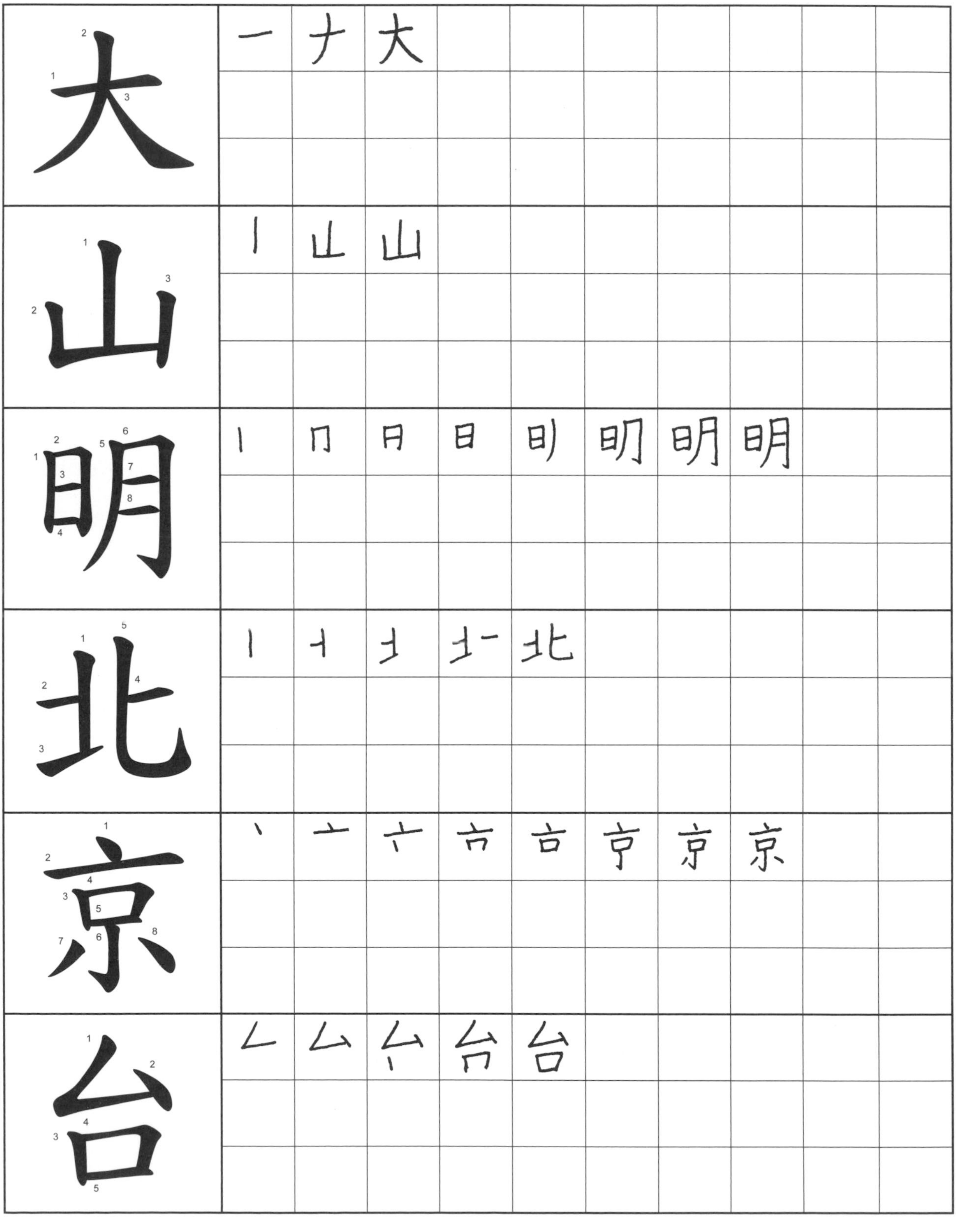

Unit A, Part 4: Character Practice Sheet (Simplified Characters)

NAME ______________________ COURSE ______________________ DATE ______________________

何	丿	亻	仁	仃	仃	何	何			
李	一	十	才	木	李	李	李			
文	丶	亠	亠	文						
生	丿	𠂉	𠂉	牛	生					
中	丨	冂	口	中						
小	亅	小	小							

Unit A, Part 4: Character Practice Sheet (Traditional Characters)

NAME ______________________ COURSE ______________________ DATE ______________________

何	丿	亻	亻一	亻丆	亻丅	亻可	何			
李	一	十	才	木	本	李	李			
文	丶	亠	方	文						
生	丿	𠂉	仁	牛	生					
中	丨	冂	口	中						
小	亅	小	小							

Unit B, Part 1: Character Practice Sheet (Simplified Characters)

NAME ______________________ COURSE ______________________ DATE ______________________

上										
海										
广										
州										
东										
人										

Unit B, Part 1: Character Practice Sheet (Traditional Characters)

NAME ______________________ COURSE ______________________ DATE ______________________

上	
海	
廣	
州	
東	
人	

Unit B, Part 2: Character Practice Sheet (Simplified Characters)

NAME ____________________ COURSE ____________________ DATE ____________________

成
都
天
津
西
路

Unit B, Part 2: Character Practice Sheet (Traditional Characters)

NAME ______________________ COURSE ______________________ DATE ______________________

成	成
都	都
天	天
津	津
西	西
路	路

Unit B, Part 3: Character Practice Sheet (Simplified Characters)

NAME ______________________ COURSE ______________________ DATE ______________________

安	安
川	川
香	香
港	港
南	南
街	街

Unit B, Part 3: Character Practice Sheet (Traditional Characters)

NAME ______________ COURSE ______________ DATE ______________

安	丶	丶丶	宀	它	安	安
川	丿	川	川			
香	丿	二	千	千	禾	禾	香	香	香
港	丶	冫	氵	氵	汁	汫	泄	洪	洪	港	港	港
南	一	十	丨	内	冇	冇	南	南	南
街	丿	彳	彳	行	行	往	往	往	往	往	往	街

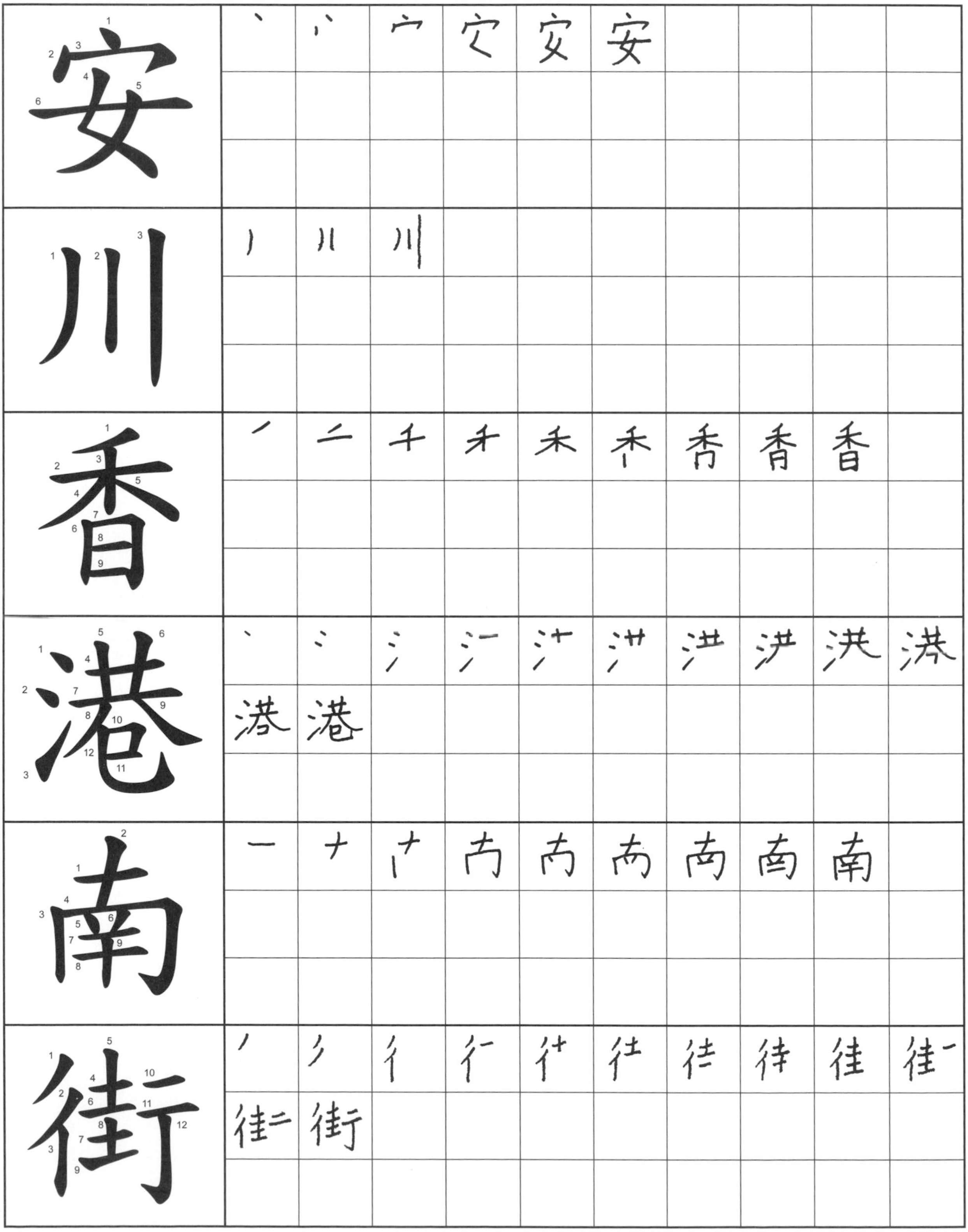

Unit B, Part 4: Character Practice Sheet (Simplified Characters)

NAME ______________________ COURSE ______________________ DATE ______________________

Character	Stroke order
河	丶 冫 氵 氵一 氵丁 氵可 河
湖	丶 冫 氵 氵一 汁 沽 湖
湾	丶 冫 氵 氵 氵亠 湾
金	丿 人 亼 今 全 金
市	丶 亠 市
省	丨 小 少 省

Unit B, Part 4: Character Practice Sheet (Traditional Characters)

NAME ____________________ COURSE ____________________ DATE ____________________

河								河		
湖										
	湖	湖								
灣										
					灣					
金								金		
市					市					
省									省	

Unit 1, Part 1: Character Practice Sheet (Simplified Characters)

NAME ______ COURSE ______ DATE ______

你	丿	亻	亻'	亻'	价	价	你		
好	𡿨	女	女	女7	好	好			
我	丿	二	手	手	我	我	我		
也	乛	也	也						
去	一	十	土	去	去				
呢	丨	冂	口	口7	口ㄱ	尸	呢	呢	

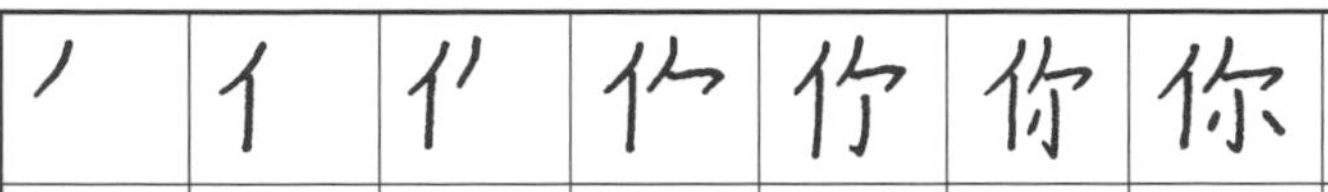

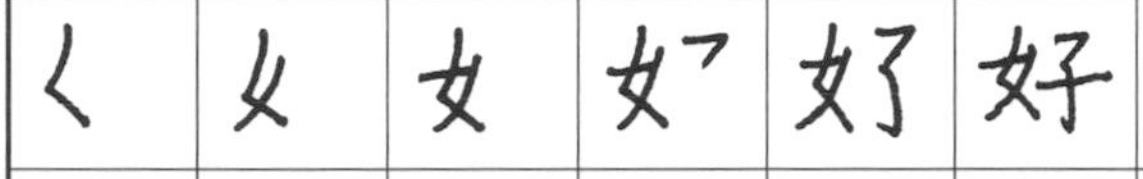

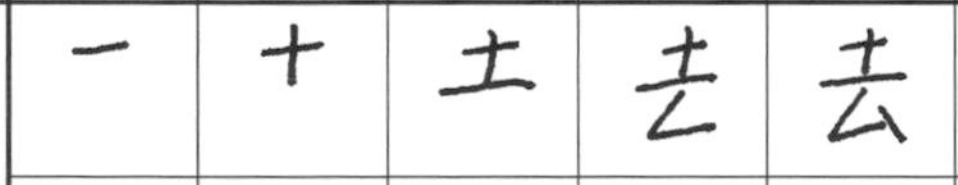

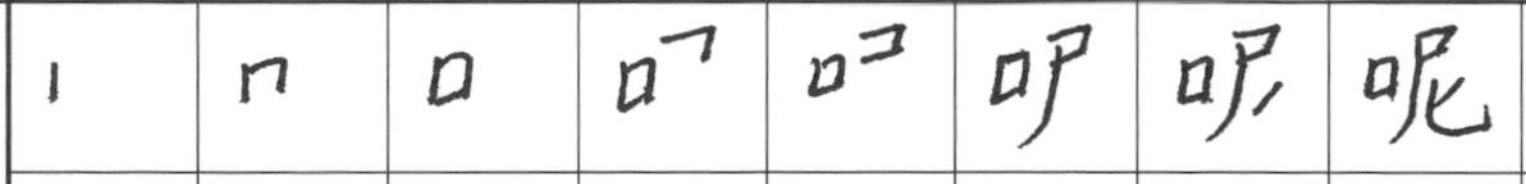

Unit 1, Part 1: Character Practice Sheet (Traditional Characters)

NAME ______________________ COURSE ______________________ DATE ______________________

你	你
好	好
我	我
也	也
去	去
呢	呢

Unit 1, Part 2: Character Practice Sheet (Simplified Characters)

NAME ____________________ COURSE ____________________ DATE ____________________

他	
她	
们	
很	
忙	
吗	

Unit 1, Part 2: Character Practice Sheet (Traditional Characters)

NAME ______________________ COURSE ______________________ DATE ______________________

他	他
她	她
們	們
很	很
忙	忙
嗎	嗎 嗎 嗎 嗎

Unit 1, Part 3: Character Practice Sheet (Simplified Characters)

NAME ______________________ COURSE ______________________ DATE ______________________

老	老
高	高
不	不
太	太
难	难
谢	谢 谢

Unit 1, Part 3: Character Practice Sheet (Traditional Characters)

NAME ______________________ COURSE ______________________ DATE ______________________

Character	Practice
老	
高	
不	
太	
難	
謝	

Unit 1, Part 4: Character Practice Sheet (Simplified Characters)

NAME ____________________ COURSE ____________________ DATE ____________________

请	
坐	
先	
走	
了	
姐	

Unit 1, Part 4: Character Practice Sheet (Traditional Characters)

NAME ____________ COURSE ____________ DATE ____________

請	請
坐	坐
先	先
走	走
了	了
姐	姐

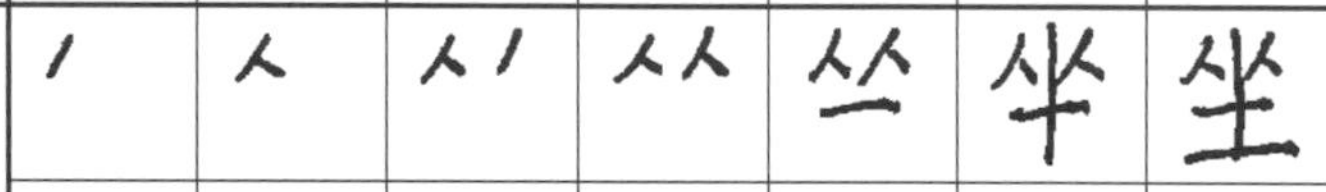

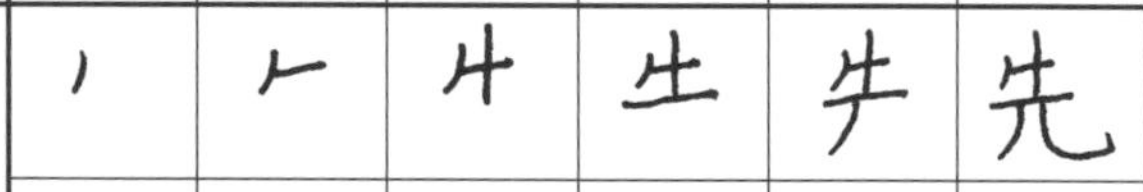

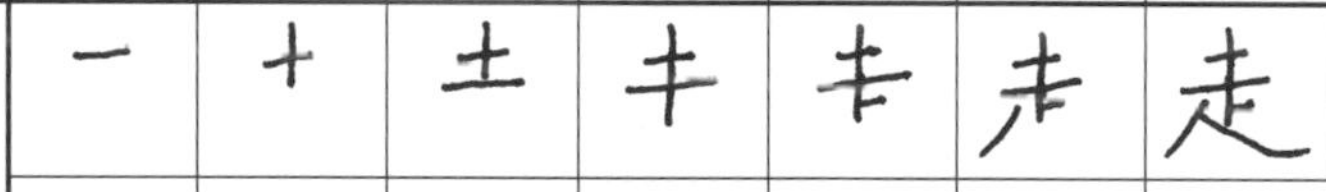

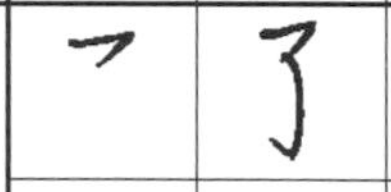

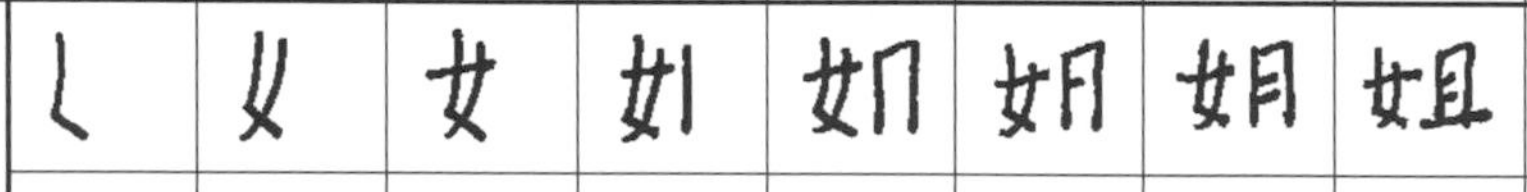

Unit 2, Part 1: Character Practice Sheet (Simplified Characters)

NAME ______________________ COURSE ______________________ DATE ______________________

哪										
国										
问										
是										
美										
叫										

Unit 2, Part 1: Character Practice Sheet (Traditional Characters)

NAME ______________________ COURSE ______________________ DATE ______________________

哪										哪
國										
	國									
問										
	問									
是									是	
美									美	
叫					叫					

Unit 2, Part 2: Character Practice Sheet (Simplified Characters)

NAME ______________________ COURSE ______________________ DATE ______________________

的	
同	
屋	
别	
名	
字	

Unit 2, Part 2: Character Practice Sheet (Traditional Characters)

NAME ________________ COURSE ________________ DATE ________________

的	ノ	亻	白	白	白	白'	的	的		
同	丨	冂	冂	同	同	同				
屋	㇕	コ	尸	尸	层	层	层	屖	屋	
別	丨	冂	口	号	另	別	別			
名	ノ	ク	夕	夕	名	名				
字	丶	丷	宀	宀	字	字				

Unit 2, Part 3: Character Practice Sheet (Simplified Characters)

NAME ______________________ COURSE ______________________ DATE ______________________

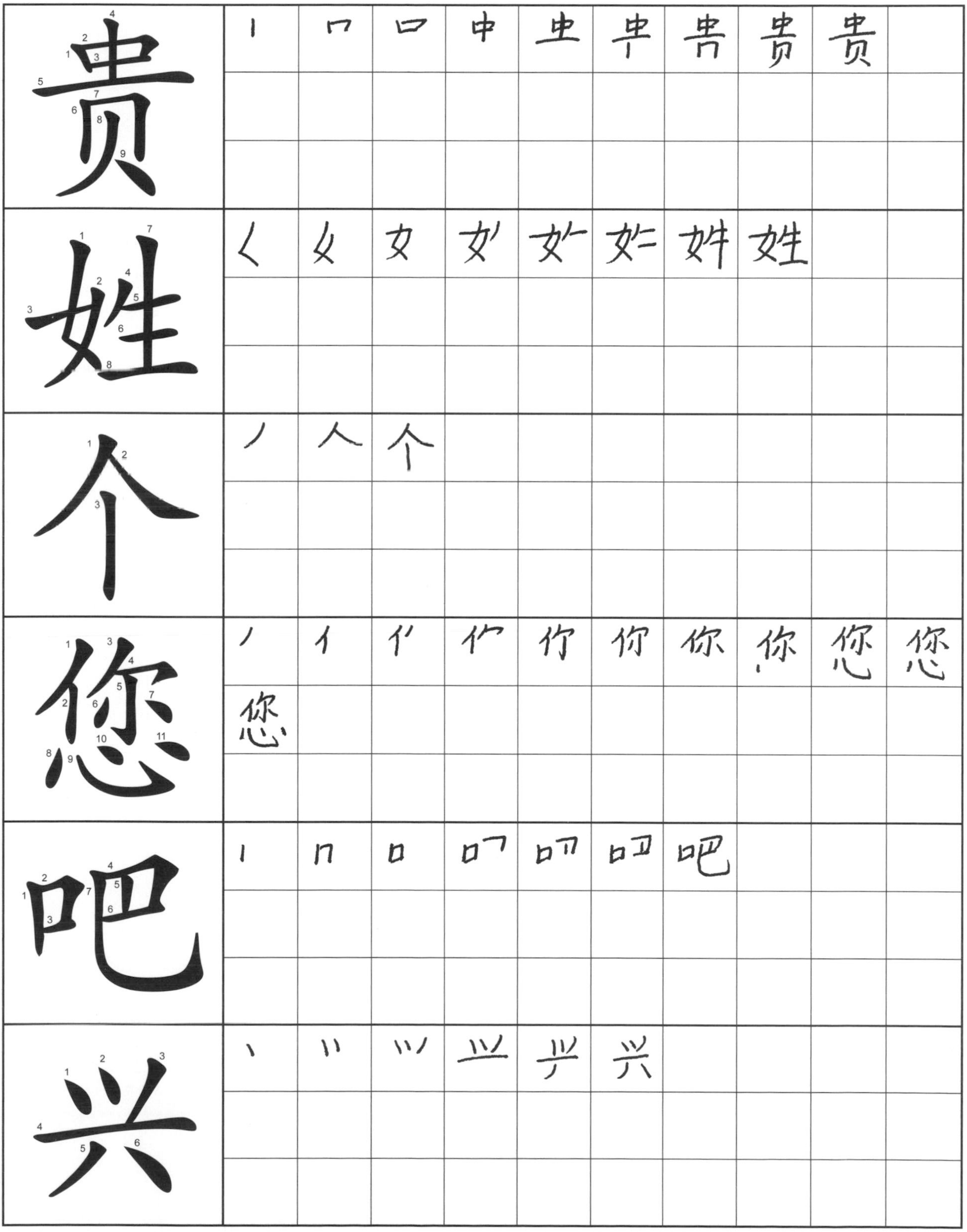

贵	
姓	
个	
您	
吧	
兴	

Unit 2, Part 3: Character Practice Sheet (Traditional Characters)

NAME ____________________ COURSE ____________________ DATE ____________________

貴
姓
個
您
吧
興

Unit 2, Part 4: Character Practice Sheet (Simplified Characters)

NAME ______________________ COURSE ______________________ DATE ______________________

片	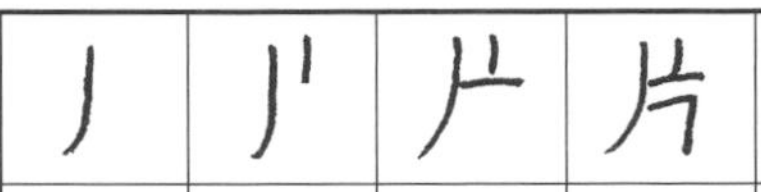
没	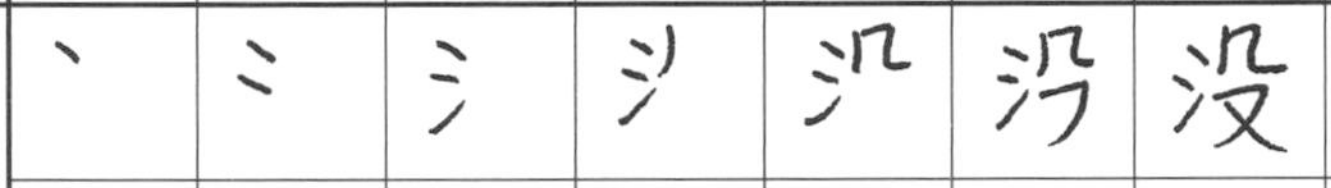
带	
公	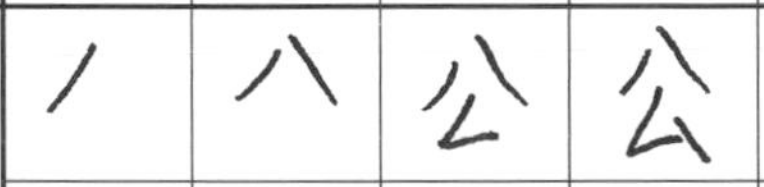
司	
这	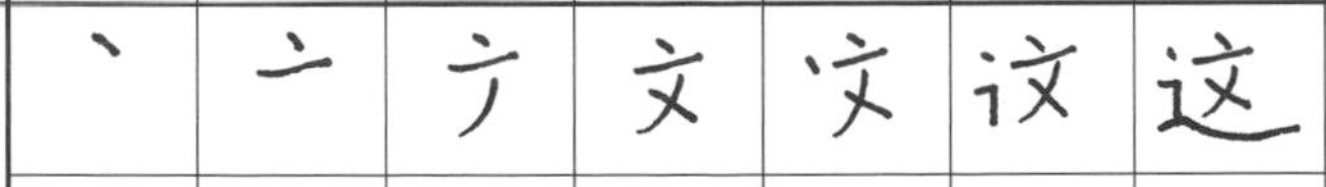

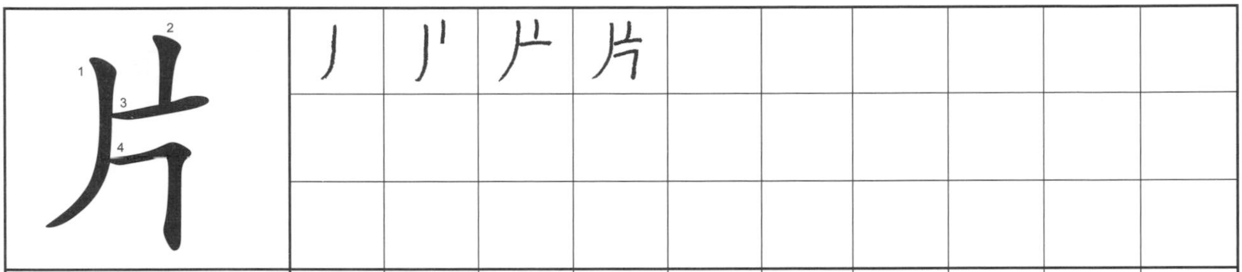

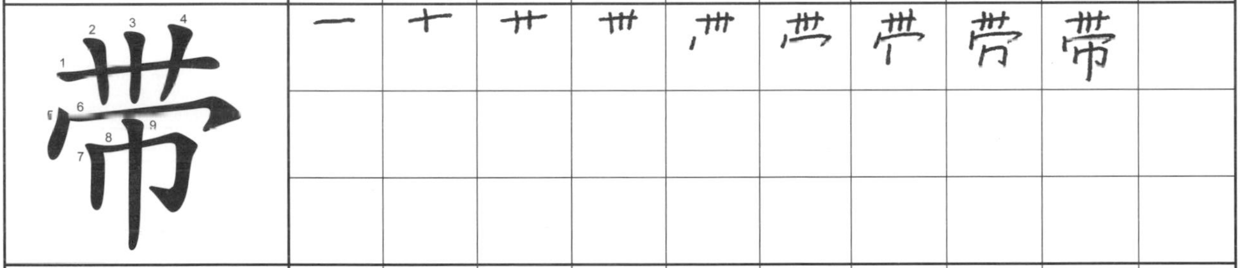

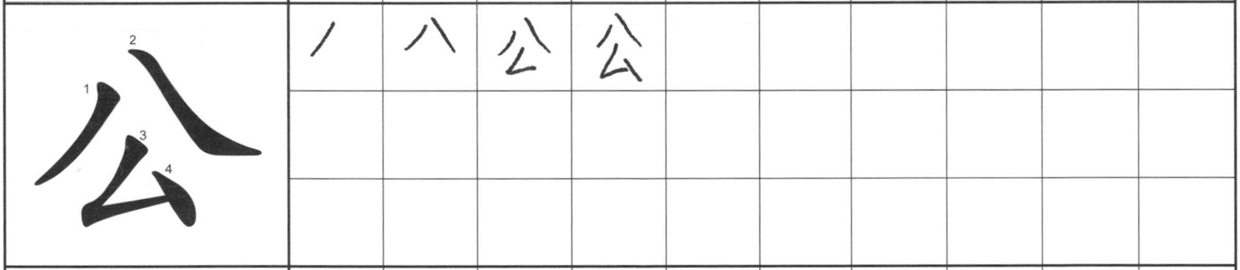

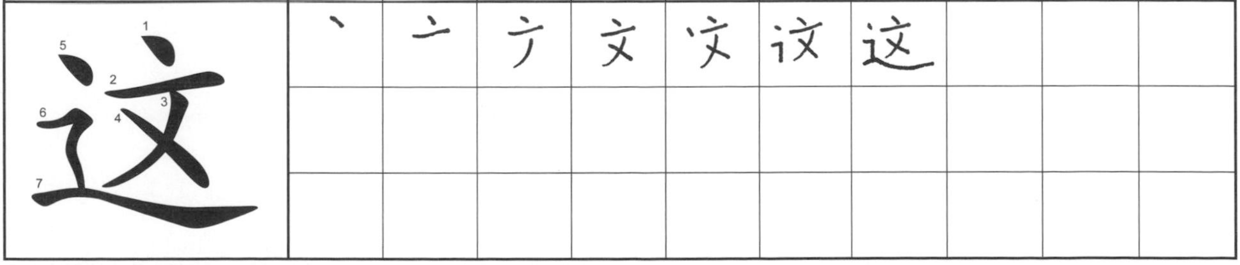

Unit 2, Part 4: Character Practice Sheet (Traditional Characters)

NAME ____________ COURSE ____________ DATE ____________

片	丿	丿丨	𠂆	片						
沒	丶	冫	氵	氵	氵	氵	沒			
帶	一	十	卄	廿	卌	卌	卌	卌	卌	卌
	帶									
公	丿	八	公	公						
司	𠃌	𠃌	司	司	司					
這	丶	亠	亠	言	言	言	言	言	言	言
	這									

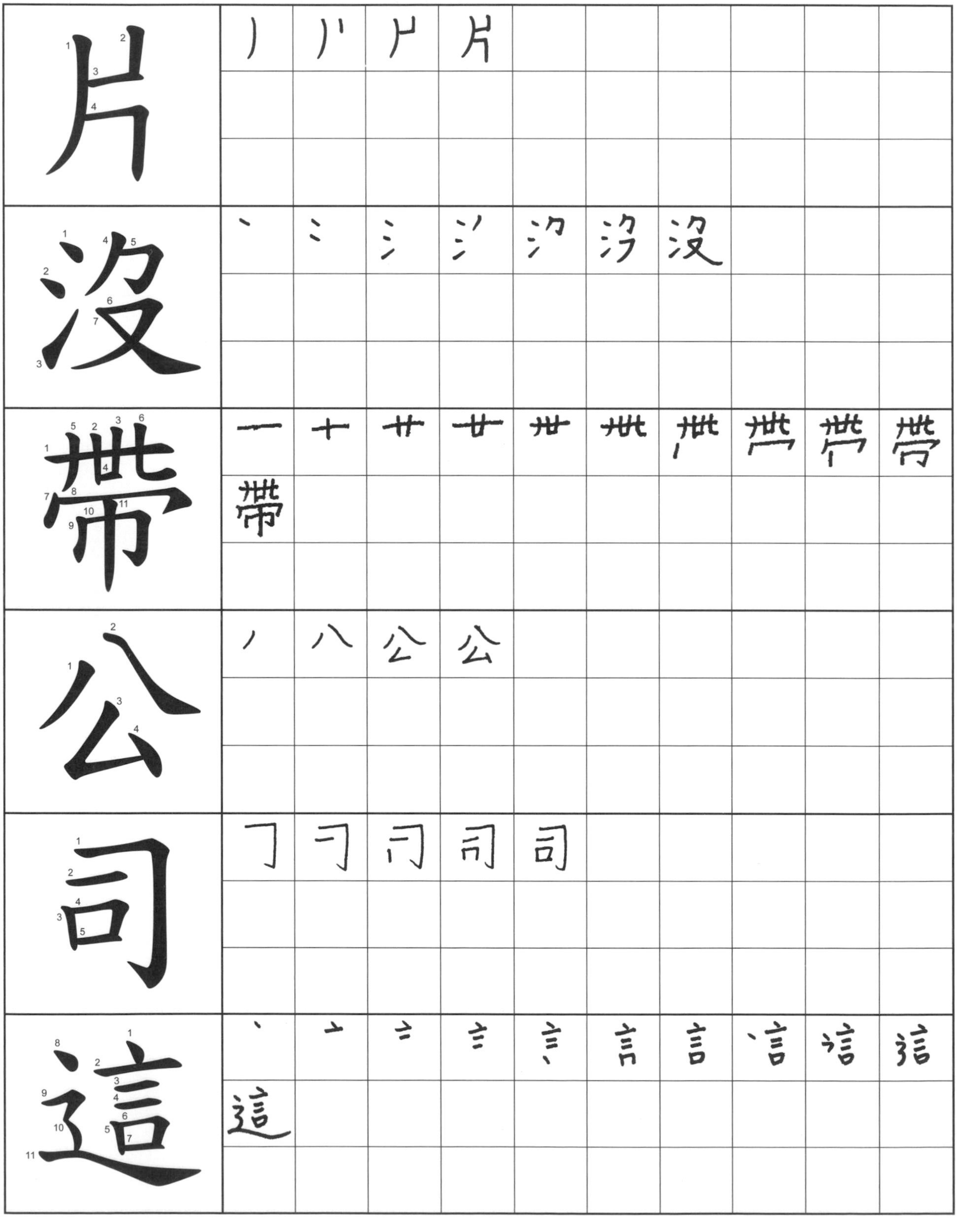

Unit 3, Part 1: Character Practice Sheet (Simplified Characters)

NAME ______________________ COURSE ______________________ DATE ______________________

Character	Stroke order
几	丿 几
位	丿 亻 … 位
两	一 … 两
男	丨 … 男
女	𡿨 … 女
师	丨 … 师

Unit 3, Part 1: Character Practice Sheet (Traditional Characters)

NAME ______________________ COURSE ______________________ DATE ______________________

幾
位
兩
男
女
師

Unit 3, Part 2: Character Practice Sheet (Simplified Characters)

NAME ______________________ COURSE ______________________ DATE ______________________

多	丿	夕	夕	多	多	多
年	丿	𠂉	仁	仁	乍	年
纪	𠃋	纟	纟	纟	纪	纪
今	丿	人	今	今		
岁	丨	山	山	岁	岁	岁
对	𠃍	又	又	对	对	

Unit 3, Part 2: Character Practice Sheet (Traditional Characters)

NAME ______________________ COURSE ______________________ DATE ______________________

多	多
年	年
紀	紀
今	今
歲	歲
對	對

Unit 3, Part 3: Character Practice Sheet (Simplified Characters)

NAME ______________________ COURSE ______________________ DATE ______________________

那						那				
少				少						
钱								钱	钱	钱
块							块			
百						百				
千			千							

Unit 3, Part 3: Character Practice Sheet (Traditional Characters)

NAME ____________________ COURSE ____________________ DATE ____________________

那	那
少	少
錢	錢
塊	塊
百	百
千	千

Unit 3, Part 4: Character Practice Sheet (Simplified Characters)

NAME ______________________ COURSE ______________________ DATE ______________________

点	
刻	
半	
差	
钟	
头	

Unit 3, Part 4: Character Practice Sheet (Traditional Characters)

NAME ______________________ COURSE ______________________ DATE ______________________

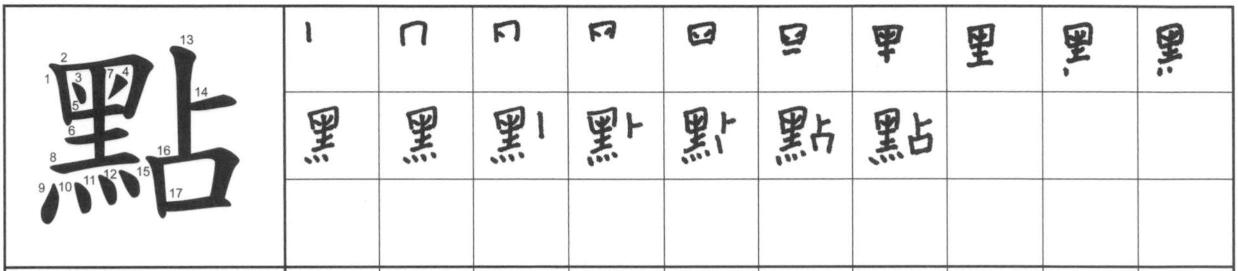

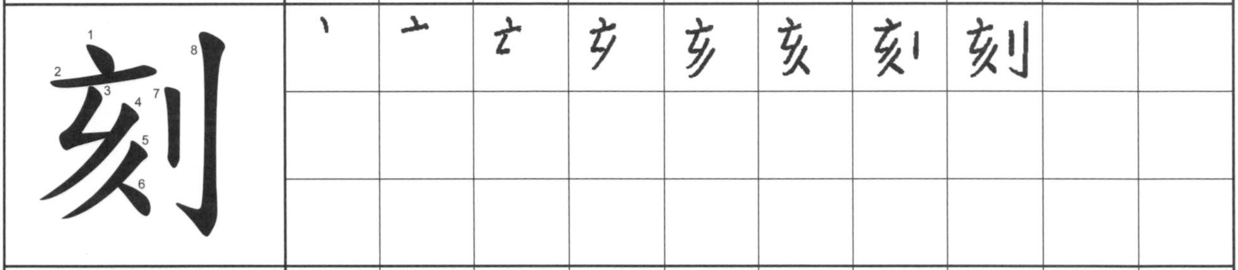

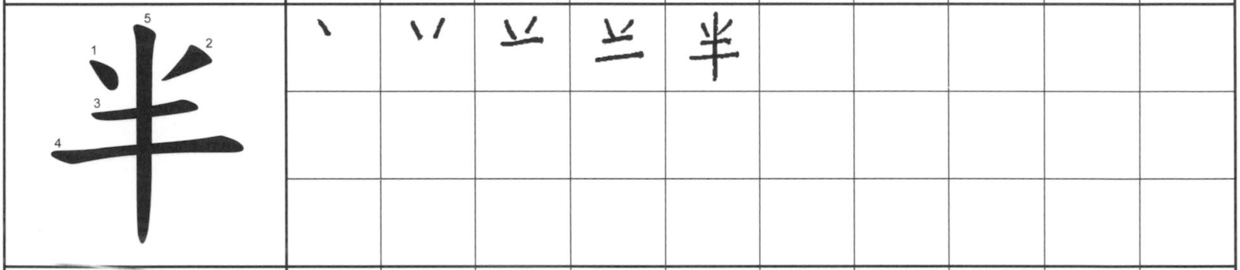

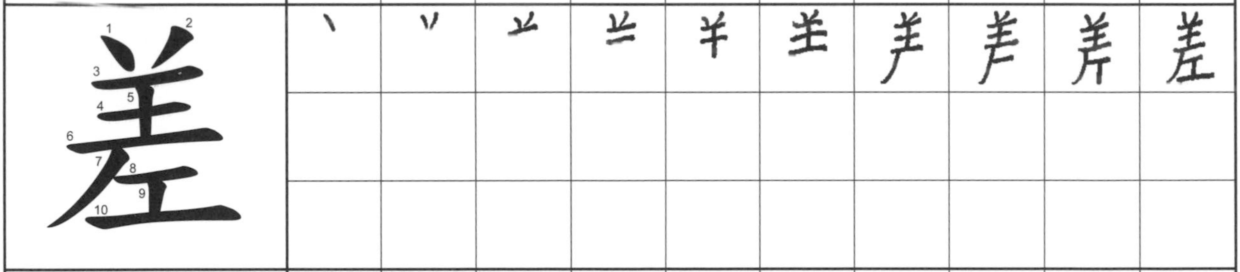

Unit 4, Part 1: Character Practice Sheet (Simplified Characters)

NAME ______________________ COURSE ______________________ DATE ______________________

开	一	二	[illegible]	开						
门	丶	[illegible]	门							
关	丶	[illegible]	[illegible]	[illegible]	[illegible]	关				
星	丨	[illegible]	[illegible]	日	[illegible]	[illegible]	[illegible]	[illegible]	星	
期	一	十	[illegible]	[illegible]	甘	其	[illegible]	其	[illegible]	[illegible]
	[illegible]	期								
谁	丶	讠	[illegible]	[illegible]	[illegible]	[illegible]	[illegible]	[illegible]	[illegible]	谁

Unit 4, Part 1: Character Practice Sheet (Traditional Characters)

NAME ____________________ COURSE ____________________ DATE ____________________

Unit 4, Part 2: Character Practice Sheet (Simplified Characters)

NAME ______________________ COURSE ______________________ DATE ______________________

什	丿	亻	亻一	什						
么	丿	𠃋	么							
就	丶	亠	亠	亠	古	亨	亨	京	京一	京𠂇
	就	就								
月	丿	冂	月	月						
号	丨	𠃍	口	口一	号					
日	丨	冂	日	日						

Unit 4, Part 2: Character Practice Sheet (Traditional Characters)

NAME ________________ COURSE ________________ DATE ________________

Character	Stroke order
什	什
麼	麻 麼
就	京 就
月	月
號	号 號
日	日

Unit 4, Part 3: Character Practice Sheet (Simplified Characters)

NAME ______________________ COURSE ______________________ DATE ______________________

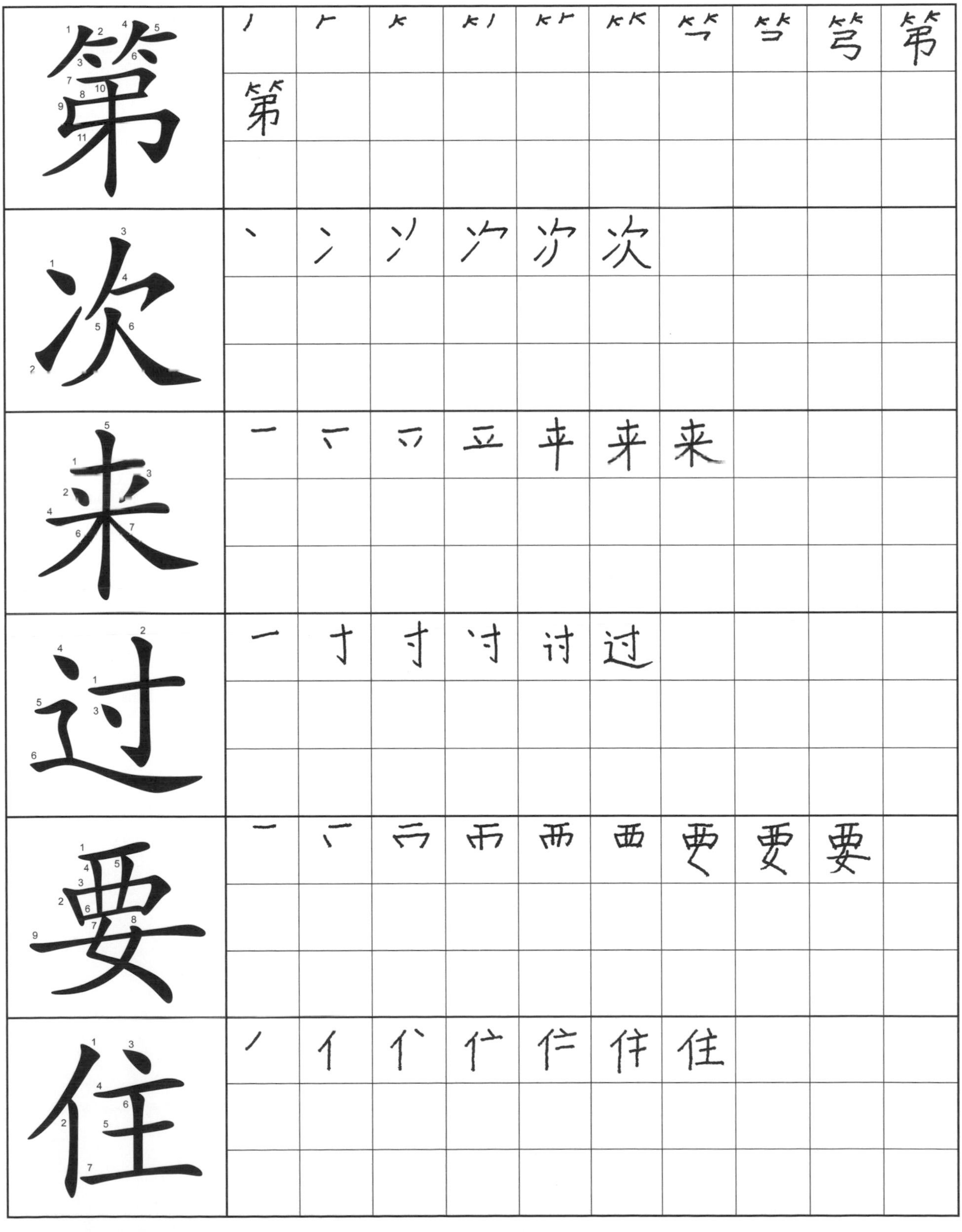

Unit 4, Part 3: Character Practice Sheet (Traditional Characters)

NAME ____________________ COURSE ____________________ DATE ____________________

第	
次	
來	
過	
要	
住	

Unit 4, Part 4: Character Practice Sheet (Simplified Characters)

NAME ______________________ COURSE ______________________ DATE ______________________

有	
口	
比	
较	
像	
万	

Unit 4, Part 4: Character Practice Sheet (Traditional Characters)

NAME ______________________ COURSE ______________________ DATE ______________________

有	有
口	口
比	比
較	較
像	像
萬	萬

Unit 5, Part 1: Character Practice Sheet (Simplified Characters)

NAME ______ COURSE ______ DATE ______

可	一	丆	冂	曰	可					
以	𠄌	𠄎	以	以						
知	丿	𠂉	𠂉	午	矢	矢	矢	知		
道	丶	丷	䒑	䒑	艹	产	首	首	首	首
	道	道								
找	一	亅	扌	扌	找	找	找			
在	一	𠂇	才	𡉀	存	在				

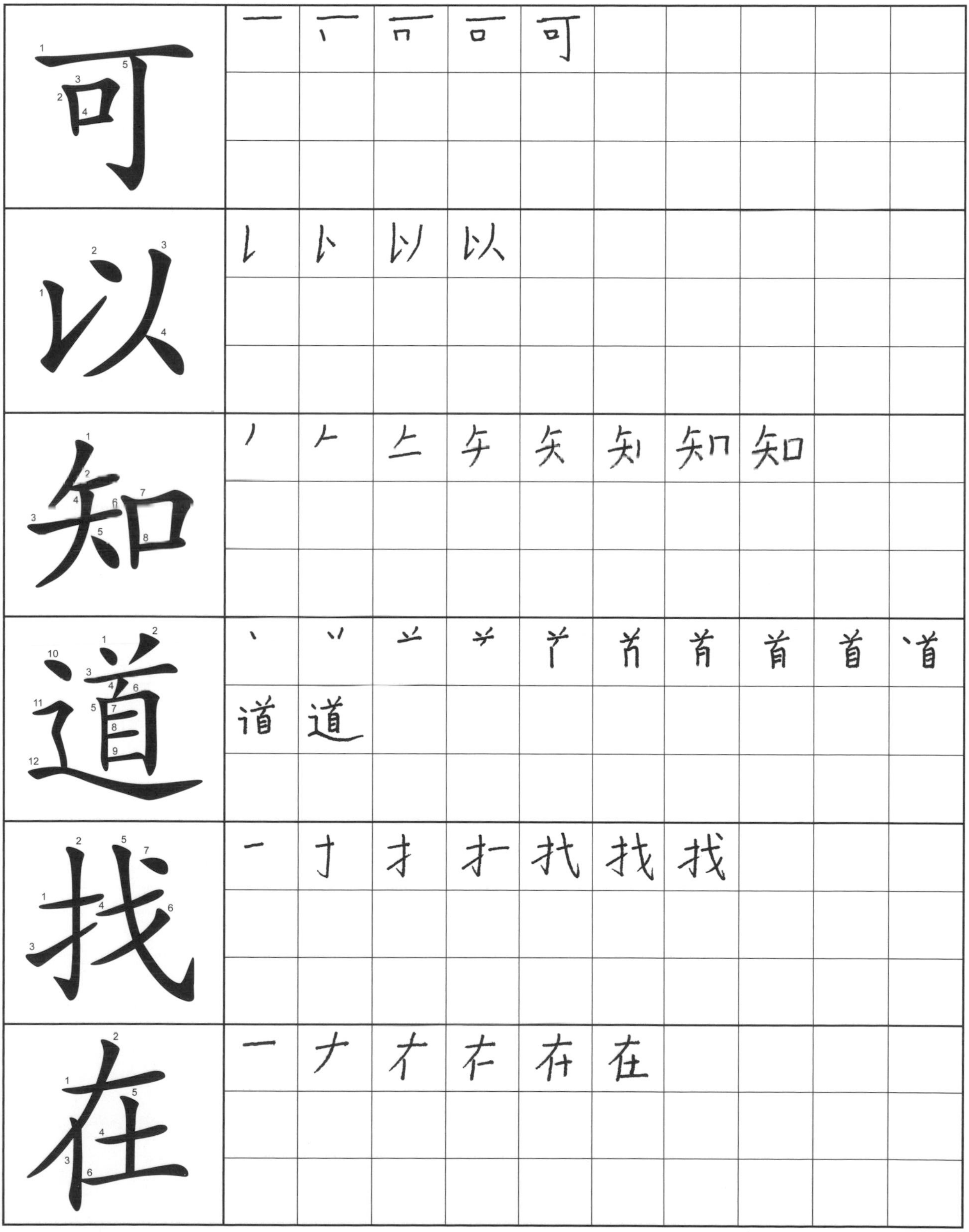

Unit 5, Part 1: Character Practice Sheet (Traditional Characters)

NAME ______________________ COURSE ______________________ DATE ______________________

可	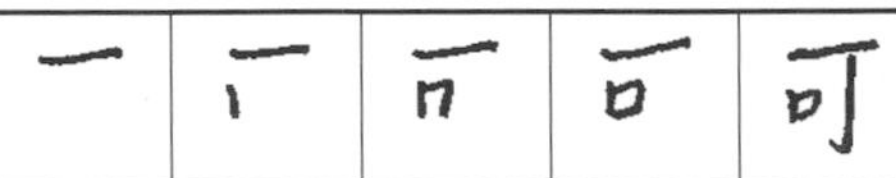
以	
知	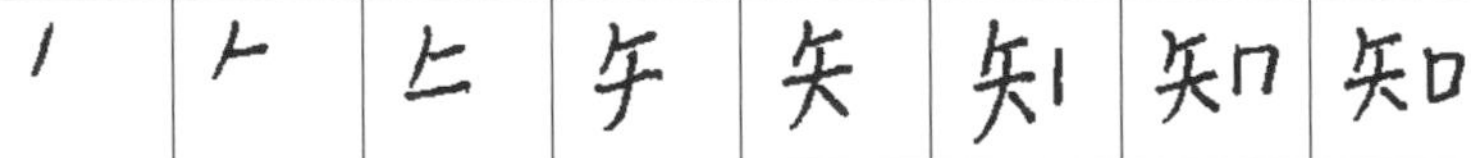
道	
找	
在	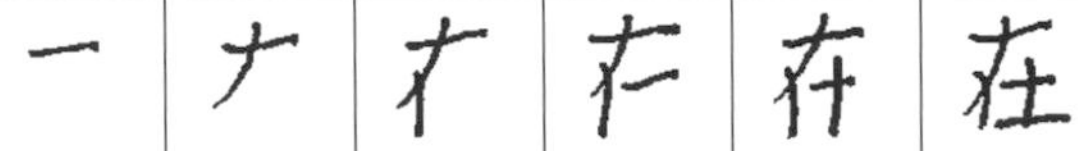

Unit 5, Part 2: Character Practice Sheet (Simplified Characters)

NAME ______________________ COURSE ______________________ DATE ______________________

吃	
饭	
学	
工	
子	
儿	

Unit 5, Part 2: Character Practice Sheet (Traditional Characters)

NAME ____________________ COURSE ____________________ DATE ____________________

吃	吃
飯	飯
學	學
工	工
子	子
兒	兒

Unit 5, Part 3: Character Practice Sheet (Simplified Characters)

NAME ______________________ COURSE ______________________ DATE ______________________

地

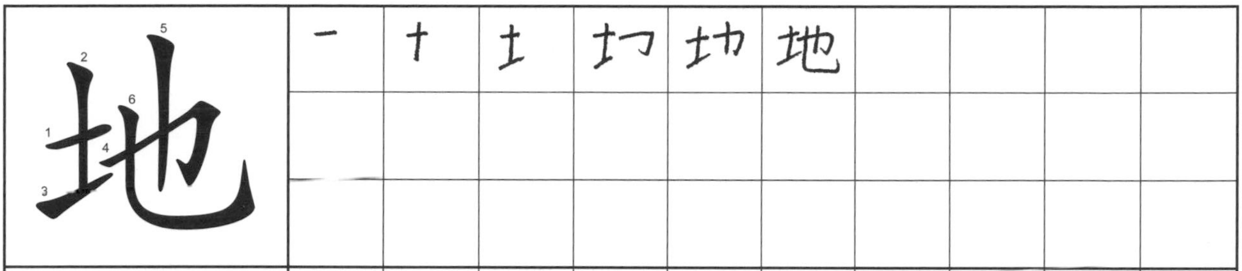

方

边

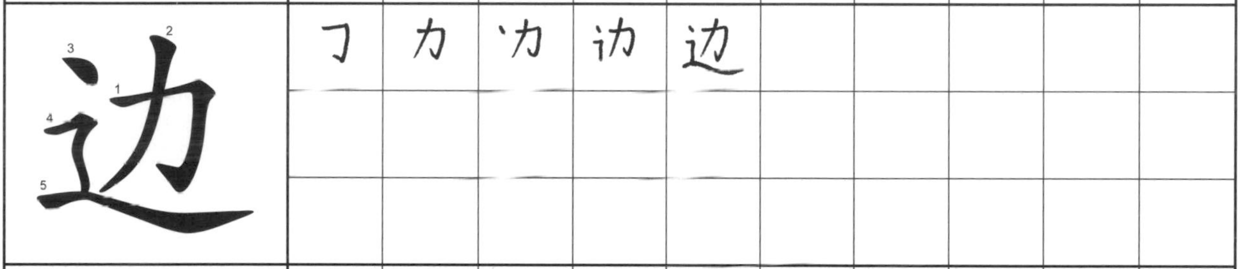

事

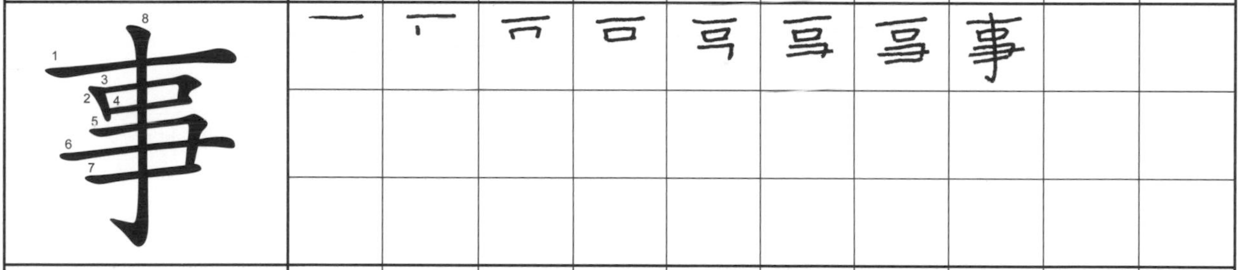

回

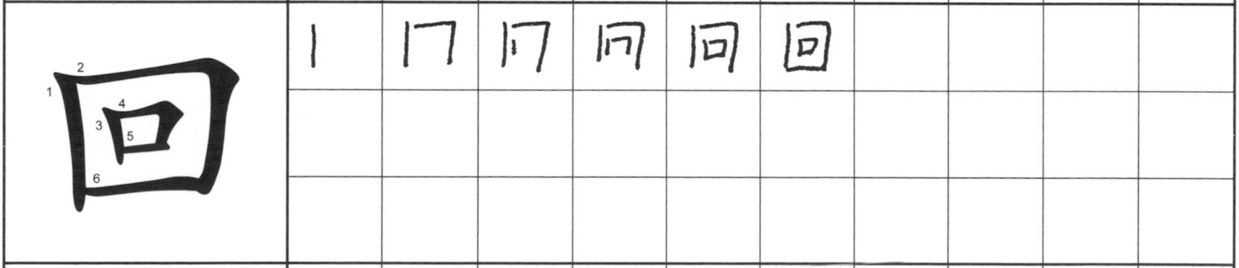

店

Unit 5, Part 3: Character Practice Sheet (Traditional Characters)

NAME ____________________ COURSE ____________________ DATE ____________________

Character
地
方
邊
事
回
店

Unit 5, Part 4: Character Practice Sheet (Simplified Characters)

NAME ______________________ COURSE ______________________ DATE ______________________

里	里
外	外
左	左
右	右
下	下
面	面

Unit 5, Part 4: Character Practice Sheet (Traditional Characters)

NAME ______________________ COURSE ______________________ DATE ______________________

裏	
外	
左	
右	
下	
面	

Unit 6, Part 1: Character Practice Sheet (Simplified Characters)

NAME ______________________ COURSE ______________________ DATE ______________________

Character	Stroke order
喜	一 十 士 士 吉 吉 吉 吉 壴 壴 喜 喜
欢	㇇ 又 又 又 欢 欢
朋	丿 ⺆ 月 月 月 朋 朋 朋
友	一 ナ 方 友
真	一 十 𠂇 冇 有 有 有 直 真 真
级	㇛ 纟 纟 纟 级 级

Unit 6, Part 1: Character Practice Sheet (Traditional Characters)

NAME ______________________ COURSE ______________________ DATE ______________________

喜	
歡	
朋	
友	
真	
級	

Unit 6, Part 2: Character Practice Sheet (Simplified Characters)

NAME ______________________ COURSE ______________________ DATE ______________________

长
看
起
轻
出
还

Unit 6, Part 2: Character Practice Sheet (Traditional Characters)

NAME ______________________ COURSE ______________________ DATE ______________________

長	長
看	看
起	起
輕	輕
出	出
還	還

Unit 6, Part 3: Character Practice Sheet (Simplified Characters)

NAME ______________________ COURSE ______________________ DATE ______________________

因	
为	
所	
作	
校	
能	

Unit 6, Part 3: Character Practice Sheet (Traditional Characters)

NAME ______________________ COURSE ______________________ DATE ______________________

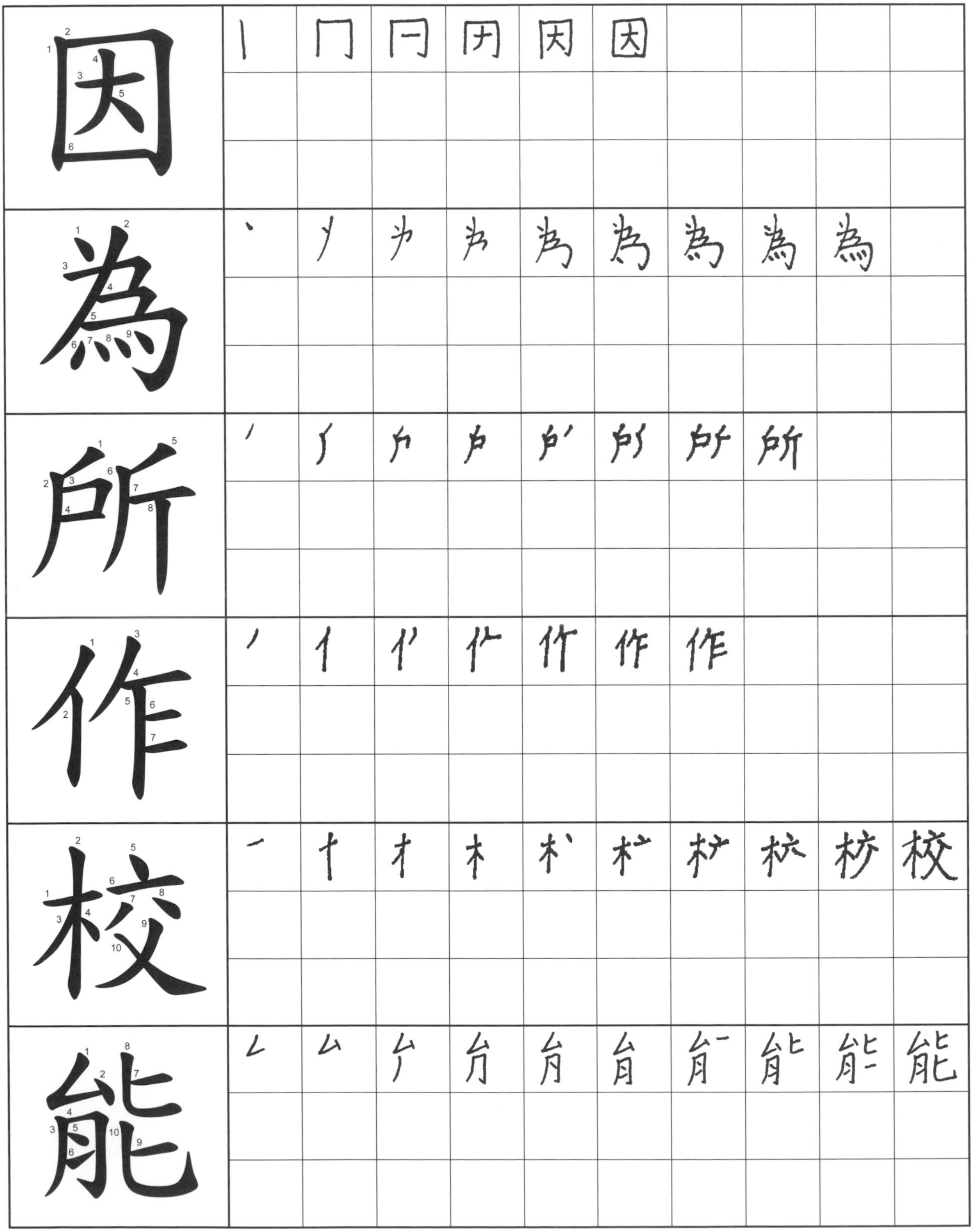

Unit 6, Part 4: Character Practice Sheet (Simplified Characters)

NAME ______________________ COURSE ______________________ DATE ______________________

哥	一	丅	𠄎	𠀀	可	哥	哥	哥	哥	哥
弟	丶	丷	当	当	弔	弟	弟			
妹	𡿨	女	女	女	女	妹	妹	妹		
忘	丶	亠	亡	亡	忘	忘	忘			
家	丶	丶	宀	宀	宀	家	家	家	家	家
给	𠃋	纟	纟	纟	给	给	给	给	给	

Unit 6, Part 4: Character Practice Sheet (Traditional Characters)

NAME ______________________ COURSE ______________________ DATE ______________________

哥					可					哥
弟							弟			
妹			女					妹		
忘							忘			
家										家
給										
	給	給								

Unit 7, Part 1: Character Practice Sheet (Simplified Characters)

NAME ______ COURSE ______ DATE ______

表	一	二	丰	主	声	耒	表	表		
县	丨	冂	冃	月	且	县	县			
城	一	十	土	圹	圻	坜	城	城	城	
原	一	厂	厂	厂	历	后	盾	原	原	原
厂	一	厂								
现	一	二	干	王	玑	玑	现	现		

Unit 7, Part 1: Character Practice Sheet (Traditional Characters)

NAME ______________________ COURSE ______________________ DATE ______________________

表	
縣	
城	
原	
廠	
現	

Unit 7, Part 2: Character Practice Sheet (Simplified Characters)

NAME ____________________ COURSE ____________________ DATE ____________________

会	会
说	说
话	话
写	写
全	全
得	得

Unit 7, Part 2: Character Practice Sheet (Traditional Characters)

NAME ______________________ COURSE ______________________ DATE ______________________

Character	Stroke order
會	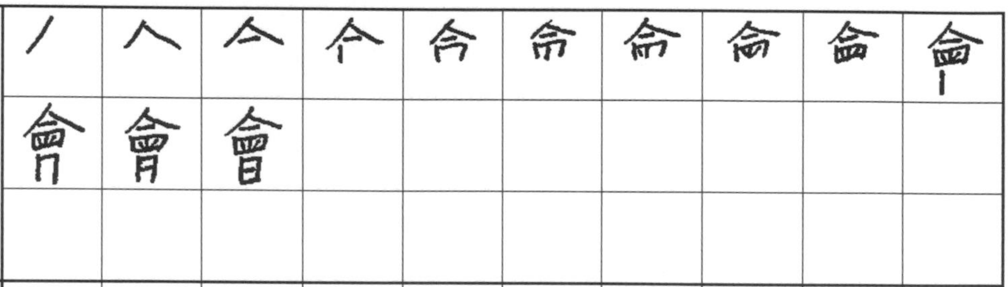
說	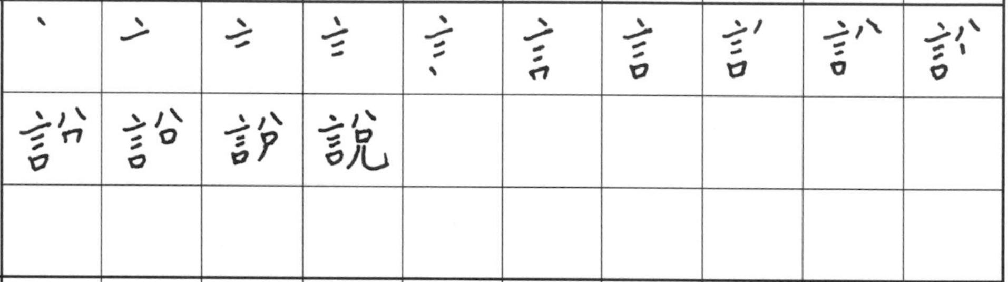
話	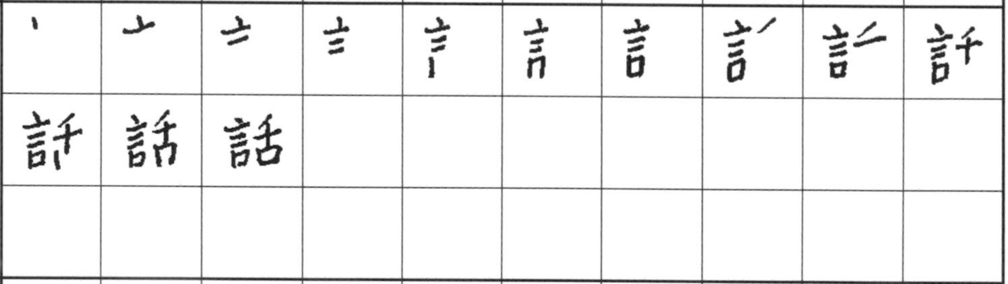
寫	
全	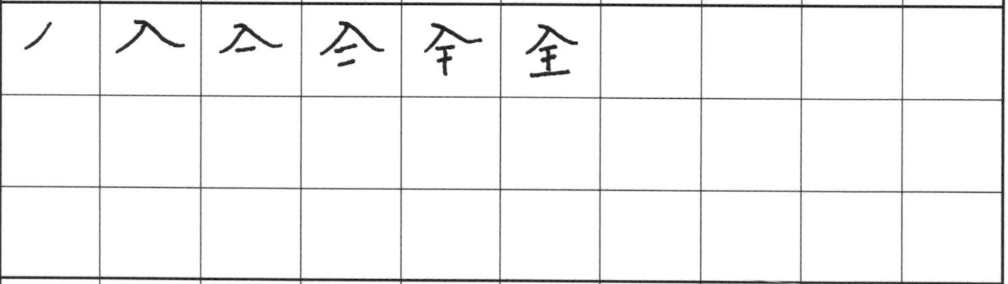
得	

Unit 7, Part 3: Character Practice Sheet (Simplified Characters)

NAME ______________________ COURSE ______________________ DATE ______________________

到	一 … 到
时	丨 … 时
候	丿 亻 … 候
始	〈 … 始
和	丿 … 和
又	フ 又

Unit 7, Part 3: Character Practice Sheet (Traditional Characters)

NAME ______________________ COURSE ______________________ DATE ______________________

Character
到
時
候
始
和
又

Unit 7, Part 4: Character Practice Sheet (Simplified Characters)

NAME ______________________ COURSE ______________________ DATE ______________________

从	丿	人	从	从						
前	丶	丷	䒑						前	
后	丿	厂				后				
之	丶		之							
听	丨		口				听			
觉	丶								觉	

Unit 7, Part 4: Character Practice Sheet (Traditional Characters)

NAME ______________________ COURSE ______________________ DATE ______________________

從	從
前	前
後	後
之	之
聽	聽 聽
覺	覺

Unit 8, Part 1: Character Practice Sheet (Simplified Characters)

NAME ______________________ COURSE ______________________ DATE ______________________

Character	Stroke order / practice
怎	怎
往	往
离	离
远	远
近	近
概	概

Unit 8, Part 1: Character Practice Sheet (Traditional Characters)

NAME ______________________ COURSE ______________________ DATE ______________________

Unit 8, Part 2: Character Practice Sheet (Simplified Characters)

NAME ______________________ COURSE ______________________ DATE ______________________

汽	丶	冫	氵	氵	汇	汽	汽			
车	一	七	乍	车						
首	丶	丷	䒑	䒑	丫	产	肖	首	首	
机	一	十	才	木	杉	机				
场	一	十	土	场	场	场				
等	丿	𠂉	⺮	⺮	⺮	⺮	竺	竺	笙	笙
	等	等								

Unit 8, Part 2: Character Practice Sheet (Traditional Characters)

NAME ____________________ COURSE ____________________ DATE ____________________

汽							汽			
車							車			
首									首	
機							機			
場										
	場	場								
等										
	等	等								

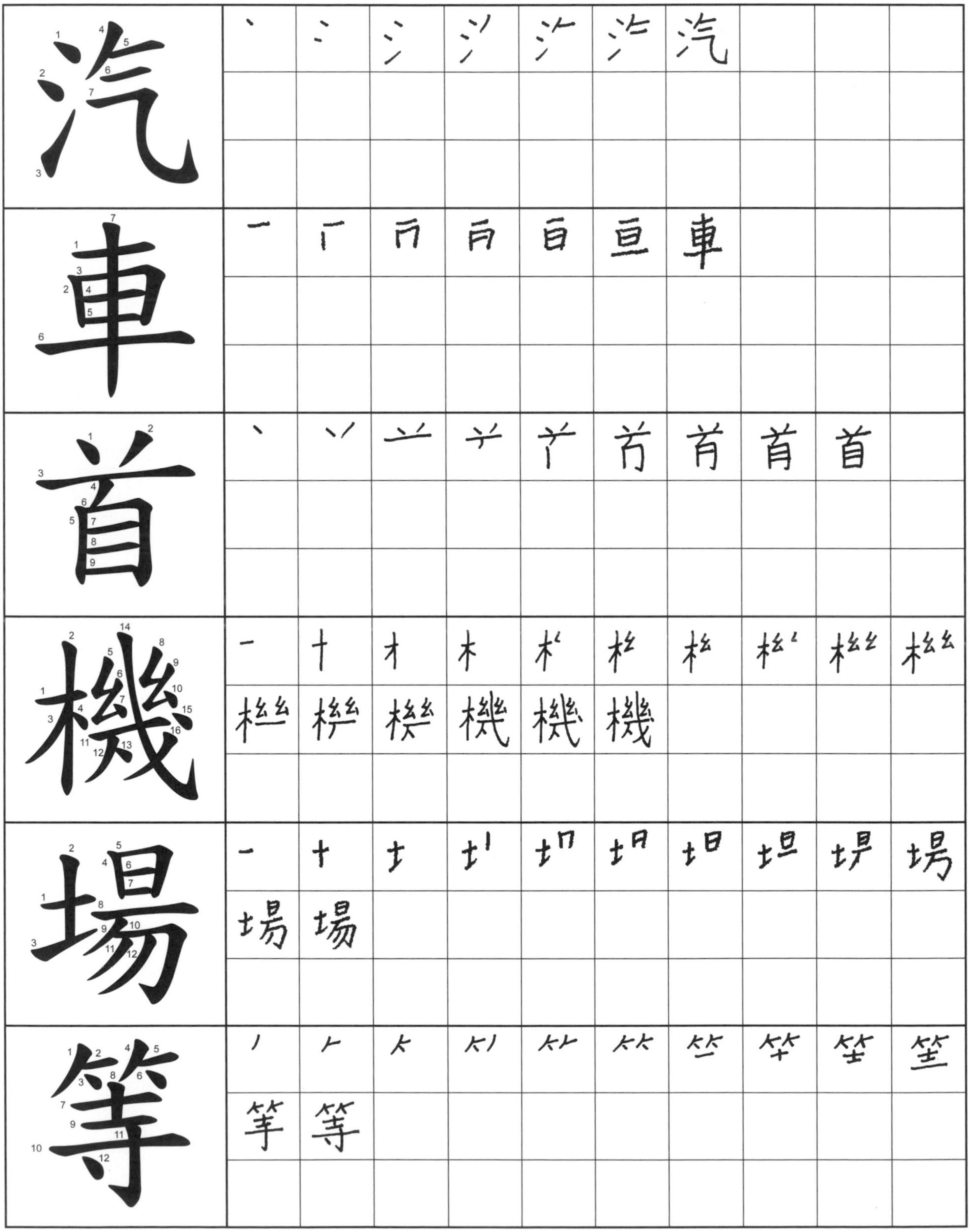

Unit 8, Part 3: Character Practice Sheet (Simplified Characters)

NAME ______ COURSE ______ DATE ______

打	一	十	扌	扌	打					
电	丨	冂	冂	日	电					
班	一	二	干	王	王	王	王	王	王	班
间	丶	丨	门	门	门	间	间			
交	丶	亠	亠	六	亣	交				
通	㇇	マ	乛	乃	丙	甬	甬	甬	诵	通

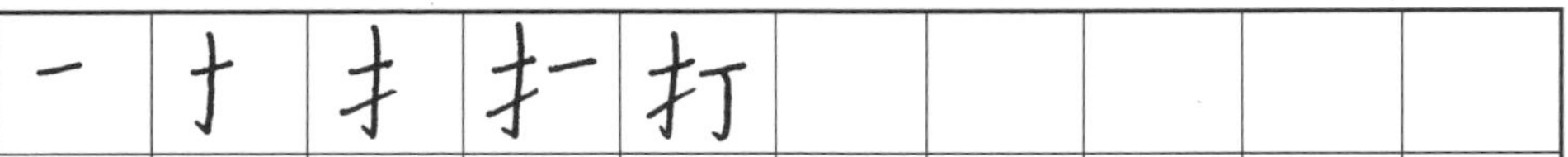

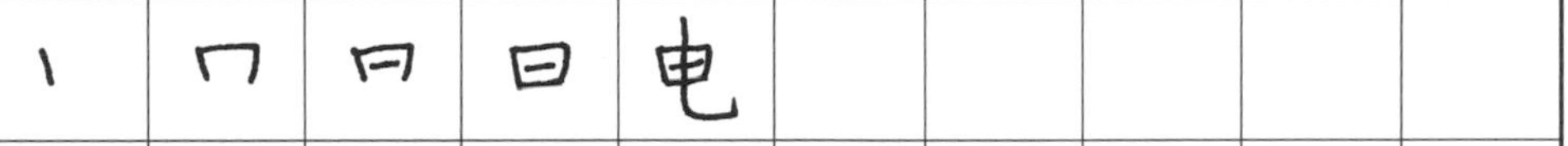

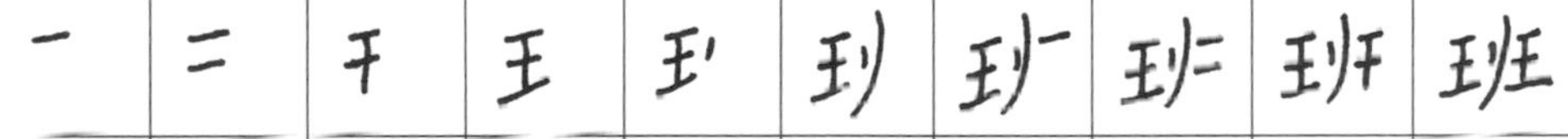

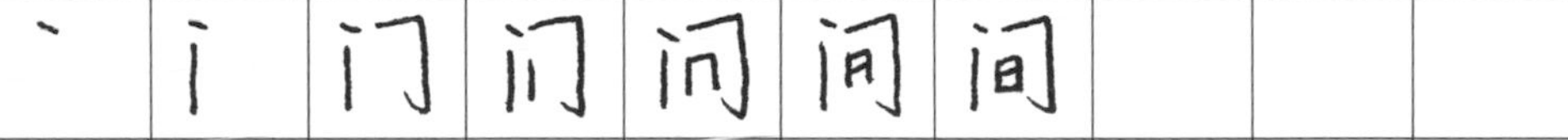

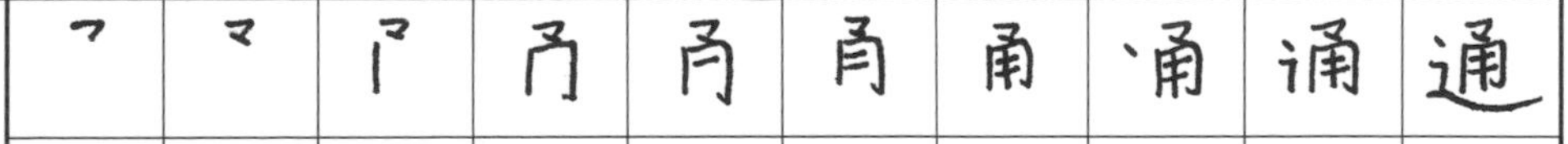

Unit 8, Part 3: Character Practice Sheet (Traditional Characters)

NAME ______________________ COURSE ______________________ DATE ______________________

Unit 8, Part 4: Character Practice Sheet (Simplified Characters)

NAME ______________________ COURSE ______________________ DATE ______________________

件	件
行	行
需	需
只	只
换	换
条	条

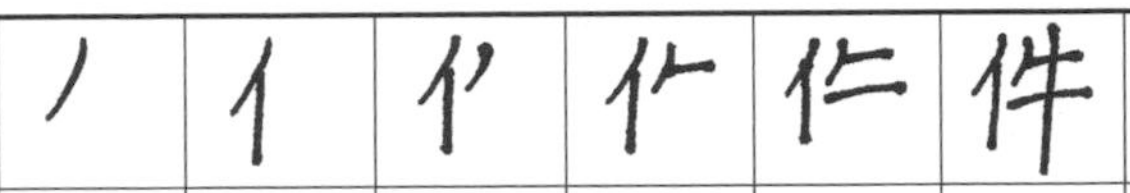

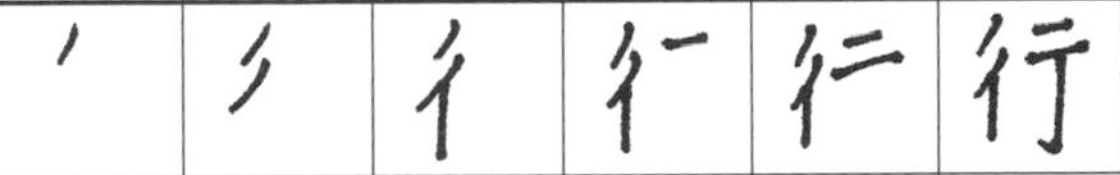

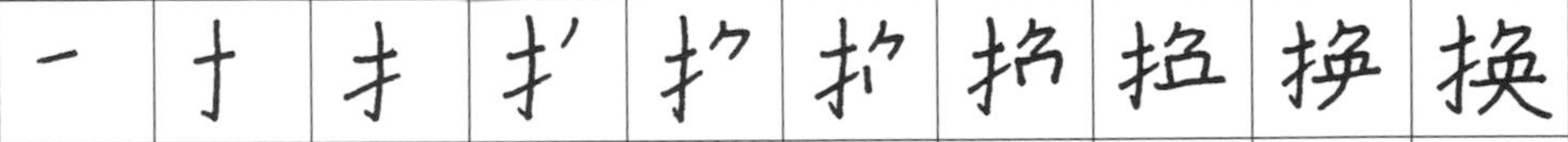

Unit 8, Part 4: Character Practice Sheet (Traditional Characters)

NAME ____________________ COURSE ____________________ DATE ____________________

件	件
行	行
需	需
只	只
換	換
條	條

Unit 9, Part 1: Character Practice Sheet (Simplified Characters)

NAME ____________________ COURSE ____________________ DATE ____________________

平	一				平					
本	一	十	才	木	本					
直	一							直		
分		八		分						
清	丶								清	清
	清									
楚	一	十	才	木		村	材	林		
			楚							

Unit 9, Part 1: Character Practice Sheet (Traditional Characters)

NAME ______________________ COURSE ______________________ DATE ______________________

平	
本	
直	
分	
清	
楚	

Unit 9, Part 2: Character Practice Sheet (Simplified Characters)

NAME ______________ COURSE ______________ DATE ______________

共	一	十	廾	廾	共	共				
站	丶	亠	亠	立	立	立	站	站	站	站
然	丿	夕	夕	夕	夕	夕	然	然	然	然
	然	然								
动	一	二	云	云	动	动				
物	丿	𠂉	牛	牛	物	物	物	物		
园	丨	冂	冂	冂	园	园	园			

Unit 9, Part 2: Character Practice Sheet (Traditional Characters)

NAME ______________________ COURSE ______________________ DATE ______________________

共	一	十	廾	廾	井	共				
站	丶	亠	亠	亣	立	立	立	站	站	站
然	丿	夕	夕	夕	夕	夕	肰	肰	然	然
	然	然								
動	丿	二	彳	台	肯	育	盲	重	重	動
	動									
物	丿	𠂉	牛	牛	牜	牞	物	物		
園	丨	冂	冂	冂	冂	冂	冂	冂	冂	冂
	園	園	園							

Unit 9, Part 3: Character Practice Sheet (Simplified Characters)

NAME ______________________ COURSE ______________________ DATE ______________________

Character	Stroke order
买	㇇ … 买
卖	一 十 … 卖
票	一 … 票
张	㇇ … 张
刚	丨 冂 … 刚
毛	丿 … 毛

Unit 9, Part 3: Character Practice Sheet (Traditional Characters)

NAME ______________________ COURSE ______________ DATE ______________

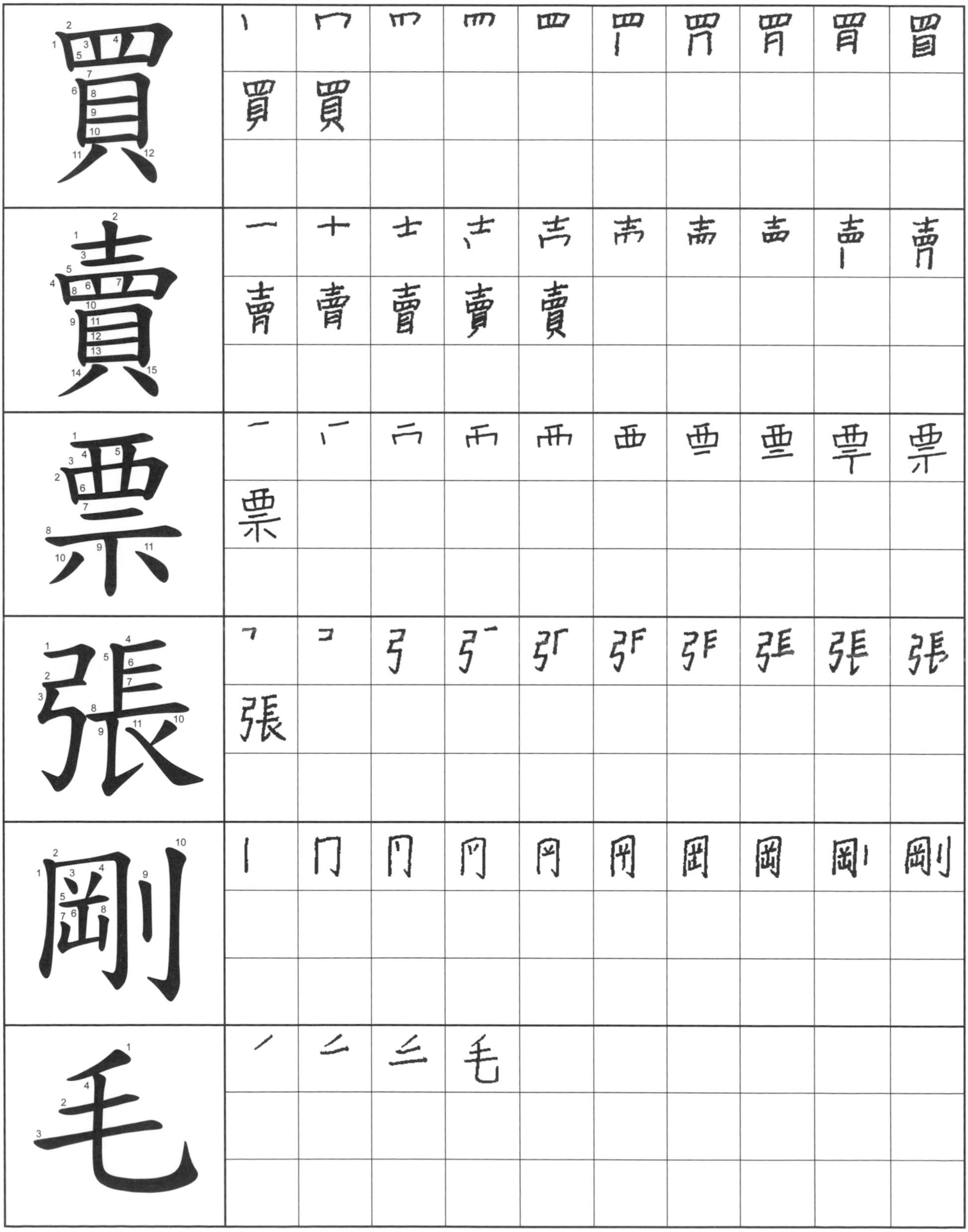

Unit 9, Part 4: Character Practice Sheet (Simplified Characters)

NAME ____________________ COURSE ____________________ DATE ____________________

早	丨	冂	日	日	旦	早				
着	丶	丷	䒑	兰	兰	𦍌	羊	着	着	着
	着									
记	丶	讠	讠	讠	记					
心	丿	心	心	心						
准	丶	冫	冫	冫	冫	冫	冫	冫	冫	准
备	丿	夕	夂	冬	各	各	备	备		

Unit 9, Part 4: Character Practice Sheet (Traditional Characters)

NAME ______________________ COURSE ______________________ DATE ______________________

早	早
着	着
記	記
心	心
準	準
備	備

Unit 10, Part 1: Character Practice Sheet (Simplified Characters)

NAME ______ COURSE ______ DATE ______

越	一	十	土	丰	丰	未	走	走	赿	越
	越	越								
最	丨	冂	日	日	旦	早	昇	昇	昇	昇
	冣	最								
温	丶	冫	氵	汀	汩	沪	泪	泪	涡	涡
	温	温								
低	丿	亻	亻	亻	仁	低	低			
度	丶	亠	广	广	庐	庐	庐	庋	度	
定	丶	丷	宀	宀	宁	宁	宇	定		

Unit 10, Part 1: Character Practice Sheet (Traditional Characters)

NAME ______________________ COURSE ______________________ DATE ______________________

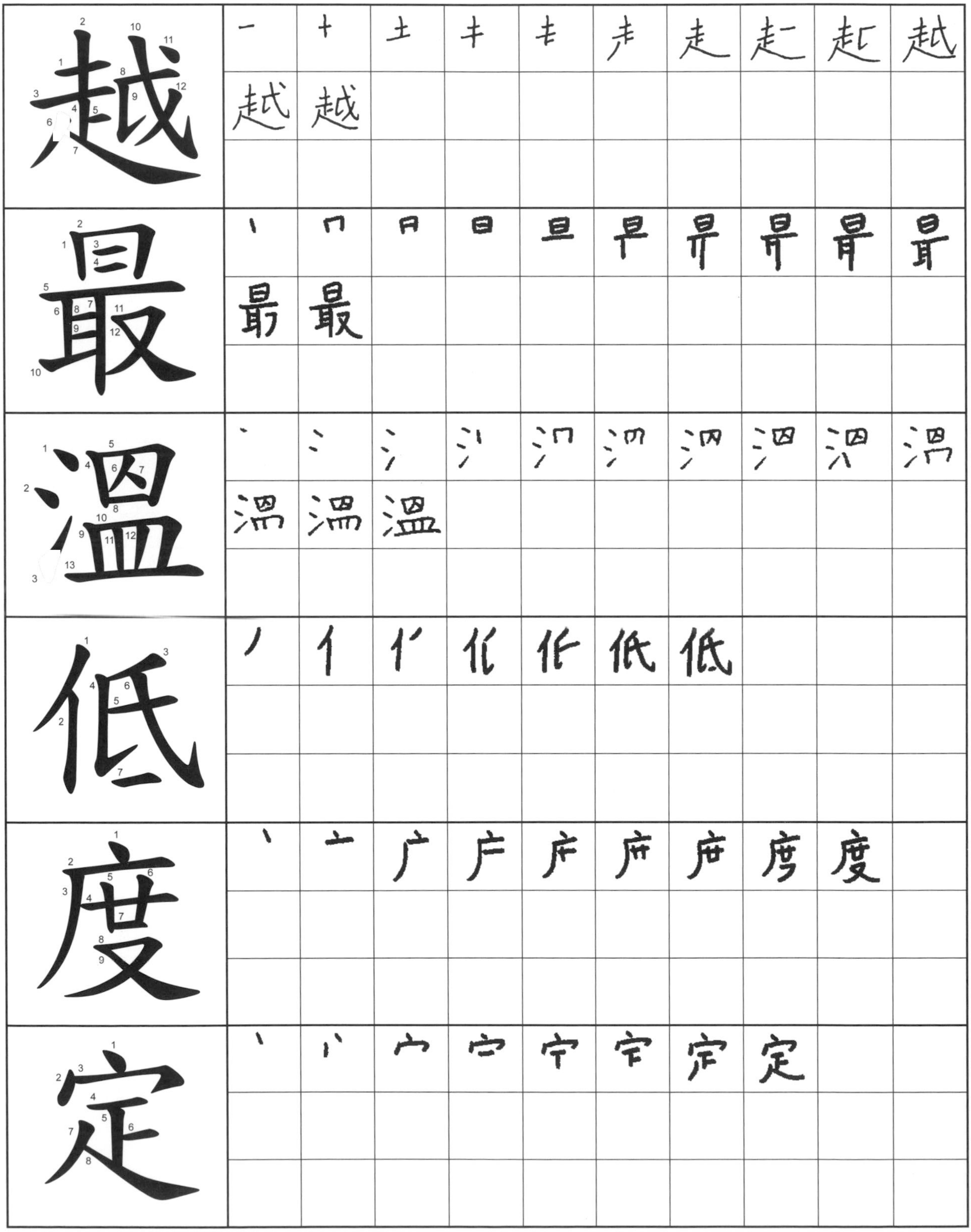

Unit 10, Part 2: Character Practice Sheet (Simplified Characters)

NAME ____________________ COURSE ____________________ DATE ____________________

气				气						
冷							冷			
热	一				执	执				热
死	一	厂	歹	歹		死				
干	一	二	干							
正	一	T	F		正					

Unit 10, Part 2: Character Practice Sheet (Traditional Characters)

NAME ____________________ COURSE ____________________ DATE ____________________

氣
冷
熱
死
乾
正

Unit 10, Part 3: Character Practice Sheet (Simplified Characters)

NAME ____________________ COURSE ____________________ DATE ____________________

样	一	十	才	木	木	木	木	栏	栏	样
进	一	二	井	井	井	讲	进			
雨	一	冂	冂	币	雨	雨	雨	雨		
但	丿	亻	亻	伯	伯	但	但			
其	一	十	廾	廾	甘	苴	其	其		
实	丶	丶	宀	宀	宀	空	实	实		

Unit 10, Part 3: Character Practice Sheet (Traditional Characters)

NAME ______________________ COURSE ______________________ DATE ______________________

樣	一	十	才	木	木'	木ᐟ	木ˇ	木ˇ	木ˇ	木ˇ
					樣					
進	丿	亻						隹	、隹	氵隹
	進	進								
雨	一	丅	冂	帀	雨	雨	雨	雨		
但	丿	亻					但			
其	一	十	廾	廾	甘	甘	其	其		
實	丶	丶	宀							
				實						

Unit 10, Part 4: Character Practice Sheet (Simplified Characters)

NAME ______________________ COURSE ______________________ DATE ______________________

岸	
错	
阳	
晚	
已	
经	

Unit 10, Part 4: Character Practice Sheet (Traditional Characters)

NAME ______________________ COURSE ______________________ DATE ______________________

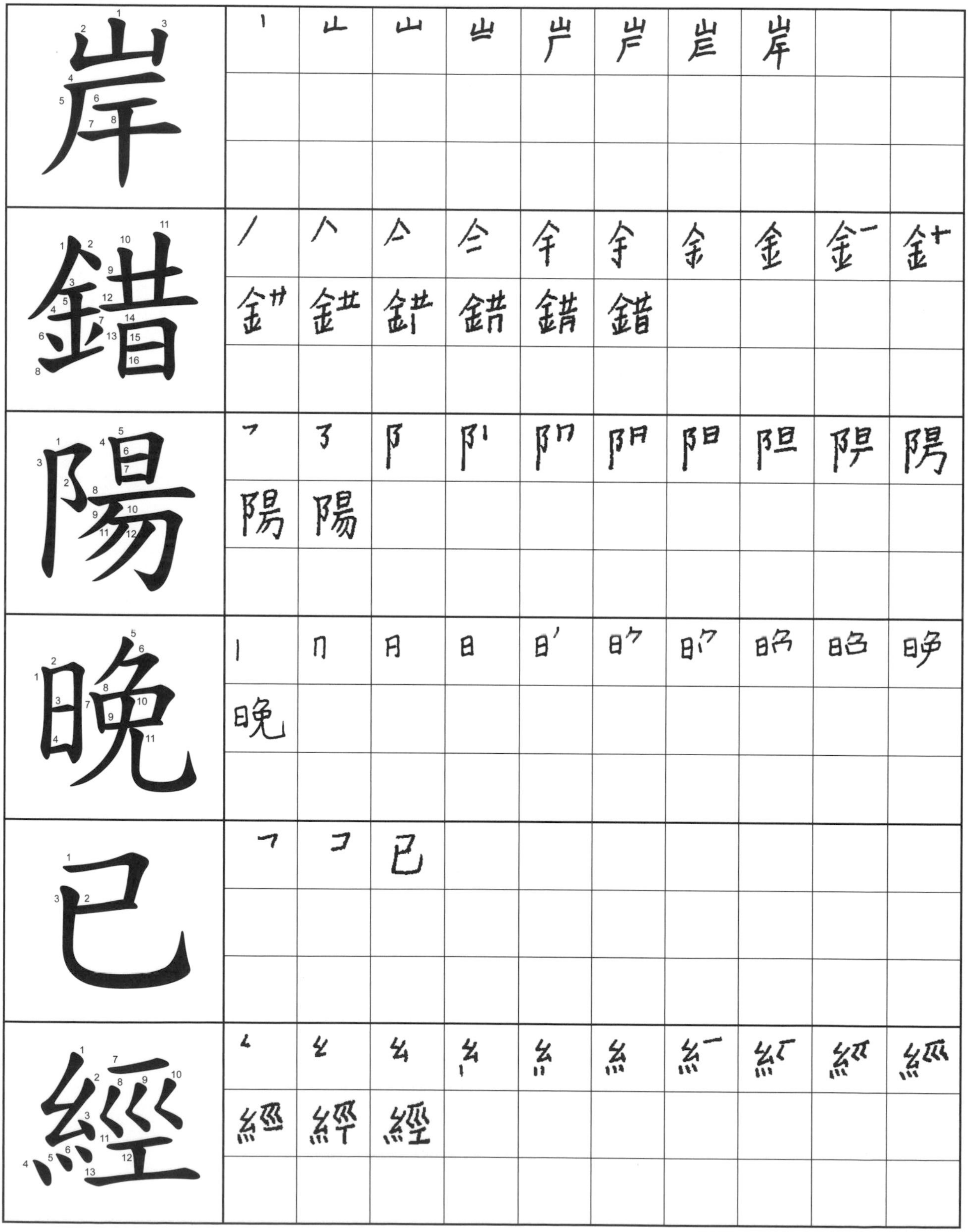

岸	岸
錯	錯
陽	陽 陽
晚	晚
已	已
經	經

Reading and Writing Exercises for *BMC Reading & Writing* Lessons A-1 to 10-4

Reading and Writing Exercises for Lesson A-1

NAME ____________ COURSE ____________ DATE ____________

A. Transcribe what you hear on the accompanying audio disc into Chinese characters.

(1)

(2)

(3)

B. Do as instructed based on the referenced part of this lesson in your textbook.

(1) Write out in Arabic numerals the telephone number listed in B1:

(2) Write out in Arabic numerals the telephone number listed in B7:

(3) Write out in Arabic numerals the telephone number listed in B10:

(4) Write in Pinyin, with tones, the surname listed in C1:

C. Miscellaneous Exercises

(1) Circle the first stroke of each character. Write that stroke on the line to the right.

三 ________ 王 ________ 五 ________

四 ________ 一 ________ 二 ________

(2) After each character, write down its total number of strokes.

二 ________ 四 ________ 一 ________

王 ________ 五 ________ 三 ________

(3) After each character, write down its pronunciation in Pinyin with tone marks.

三 ________ 二 ________ 王 ________

一 ________ 四 ________ 五 ________

(4) After each character, write down an English translation.

四 ________ 一 ________ 二 ________

五 ________ 三 ________ 王 ________

Reading and Writing Exercises for Lesson A-2

NAME ______________________ COURSE ______________ DATE ______________

A. Transcribe what you hear on the accompanying audio disc into Chinese characters.

(1)

(2)

(3)

B. Do as instructed based on the referenced part of this lesson in your textbook.

(1) Write out in Arabic numerals the telephone number listed in B3:

(2) Write out in Arabic numerals the telephone number listed in B5:

(3) If you saw the numbers given in C2 on a class schedule, what would they mean?

(4) Write in Pinyin, with tones, the surname in D1 followed by the surname in D2:

C. Miscellaneous Exercises

(1) Write the following telephone numbers in Chinese characters.

57241928 ______________________________

74243561 ______________________________

25387694 ______________________________

(2) Write your current telephone number in Chinese characters.

____

(3) Complete the following numerical sequences by writing in the appropriate Chinese characters.

a) 一二三____五六____八____十

b) 十九____七____五四____二一

c) 一____三____五____七____九____

d) 十____八____六____四____二____

e) 一三五 ____ ____

f) 十八六 ____ ____

Reading and Writing Exercises for Lesson A-3

NAME ____________________ COURSE ____________________ DATE ____________________

A. Transcribe what you hear on the accompanying audio disc into Chinese characters.

(1)

(2)

(3)

B. Do as instructed based on the referenced part of this lesson in your textbook.

(1) Write out in Pinyin, with tones, the personal name listed in A2:

(2) Write out in Pinyin, with tones, the personal name listed in A9:

(3) Write out in Pinyin, with tones, the place name listed in B1:

(4) Write out in Pinyin, with tones, the place name listed in B2:

C. Elevator Exercise

The following was adapted from a sign in an elevator in an apartment building in Hong Kong (it's in traditional characters, but that won't affect your ability to complete this exercise, even if you're studying only simplified characters):

八樓	林大山
七樓	王明
六樓	白亞權
五樓	王立
四樓	李大明
三樓	林玉玲
二樓	王大鵬
地下	
大門	

Based on the information in the sign, answer the questions below (we realize some of the characters above haven't been introduced yet, but use what you know to help you figure out the meaning of what you don't know).

(1) On which floor does Lin Yuling live? ____________________

(2) On which floor does Wang Dapeng live? ____________________

(3) On which floor does Bai Yaquan live? ____________________

(4) On which floor does Li Daming live? ____________________

(5) On which floor does Wang Li live? ____________________

(6) Who lives on the eighth floor? ____________________

(7) Who lives on the seventh floor? ____________________

(8) What do you think the character 樓 (pronounced **lóu**, written 楼 in simplified characters) means? ____________________

Reading and Writing Exercises for Lesson A-4

NAME ______________________ COURSE ______________ DATE ______________

A. Transcribe what you hear on the accompanying audio disc into Chinese characters.

(1)

(2)

(3)

B. Do as instructed based on the referenced part of this lesson in your textbook.

(1) Write out in Pinyin, with tones, the personal name listed in A1:

(2) Write out in Pinyin, with tones, the personal name listed in B2:

(3) Write out in Pinyin, with tones, the place name listed in C3:

(4) Write out in Pinyin, with tones, the place name listed in C4:

C. Map Reading Exercise

(1) After each Chinese place name at the bottom of this page, write the corresponding Pinyin, with tones, followed by the place's coordinates on the map (give the coordinates in the form A-1, etc.). All of these places exist, but a few of them are smaller and not so well known.

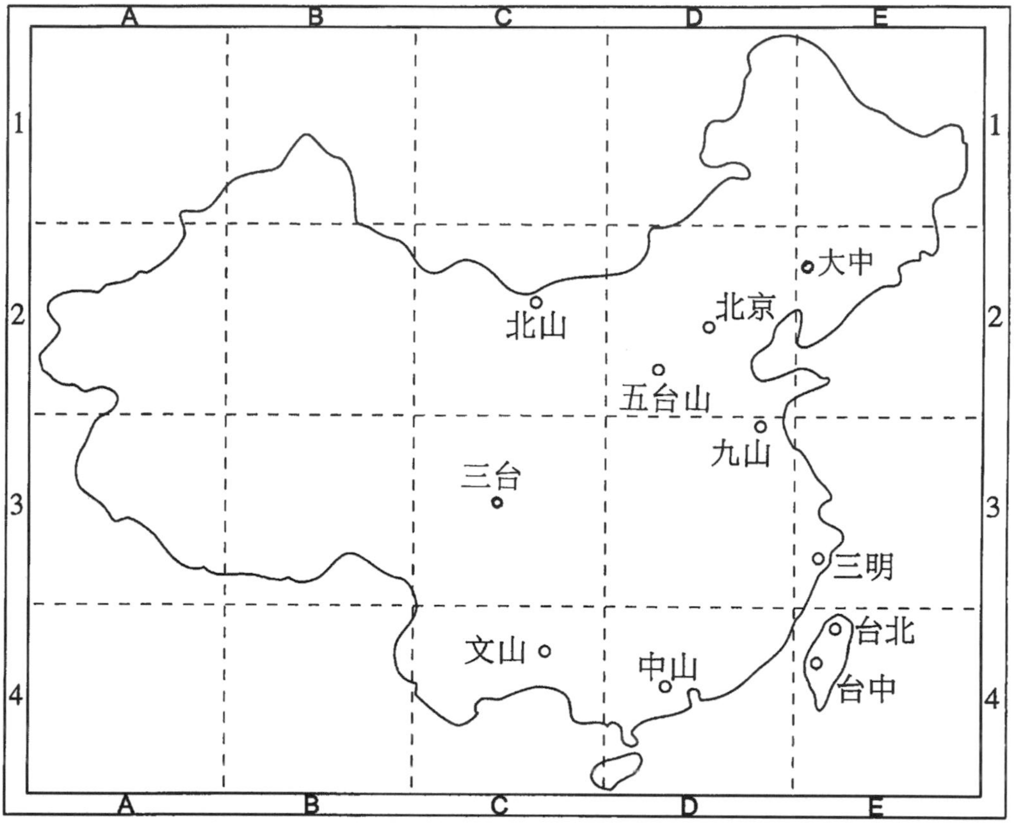

北京 ______________________ 台北 ______________________

三明 ______________________ 文山 ______________________

三台 ______________________ 九山 ______________________

北山 ______________________ 台中 ______________________

中山 ______________________ 大中 ______________________

五台山 ____________________

Reading and Writing Exercises for Lesson B-1

NAME ____________________ COURSE ____________________ DATE ____________________

A. Transcribe what you hear on the accompanying audio disc into Chinese characters.

(1)

(2)

(3)

B. Do as instructed based on the referenced part of this lesson in your textbook.

(1) Write out in Pinyin, with tones, the personal name listed in A3:

(2) Write out in Pinyin, with tones, the place name listed in B2:

(3) Write out in Pinyin, with tones, what is written in C2:

(4) Write out in Pinyin, with tones, what is written in C4:

C. Miscellaneous Exercises

(1) Circle the first stroke of each character. Write that stroke on the line to the right.

上 ________ 人 ________ 州 ________

海 ________ 东 (東) ________ 广 (廣) ________

(2) After each character, write down its total number of strokes.

大 ________ 文 ________ 六 ________

林 ________ 何 ________ 山 ________

(3) After each character, write down its pronunciation in Pinyin with tone marks.

十 ________ 京 ________ 生 ________

李 ________ 八 ________ 台 ________

(4) After each character, write down an English translation.

北 ________ 小 ________ 七 ________

九 ________ 明 ________ 中 ________

Reading and Writing Exercises for Lesson B-2

NAME ____________________ COURSE ____________________ DATE ____________________

A. Transcribe what you hear on the accompanying audio disc into Chinese characters.

(1)

(2)

(3)

B. Do as instructed based on the referenced part of this lesson in your textbook.

(1) Write out in Pinyin, with tones, the personal name listed in A1:

(2) Write out in Pinyin, with tones, the place name listed in B2:

(3) Write out in Pinyin, with tones, what is written in C3:

(4) Write out in Pinyin, with tones, what is written in C4:

C. Building Directory Exercise

You see the following directory inside a condominium in Taipei (it's in traditional characters, but that won't affect your ability to complete this exercise):

一二四	王小文
一二五	李大林
一二六	張海雲
二三五	梅文中
二三六	何西天
三八七	李山山

三八八	林生明
三八九	路汀生
五四四	李香雲
五四五	何大生
五四六	王文林

Based on the information above, answer the questions below (if asked for people's names, give their whole names).

(1) Who lives in apartment number 388? ________________

(2) Who lives in apartment number 236? ________________

(3) Who lives in apartment number 125? ________________

(4) Who lives in apartment number 387? ________________

(5) Who lives in apartment number 124? ________________

(6) Who lives in apartment number 545? ________________

(7) In which apartment does Li Xiangyun live? ________________

(8) In which apartment does Lu Tingsheng live? ________________

(9) On which floor does Zhang Haiyun live? ________________

(10) On which floor does Mei Wenzhong live? ________________

Reading and Writing Exercises for Lesson B-3

NAME ______________________ COURSE ______________________ DATE ______________________

A. Transcribe what you hear on the accompanying audio disc into Chinese characters.

(1)

(2)

(3)

B. Do as instructed based on the referenced part of this lesson in your textbook.

(1) Write out in Pinyin, with tones, the personal name listed in A6:

(2) Write out in Pinyin, with tones, the place name listed in B4:

(3) Write out in Pinyin, with tones, what is written in C1:

(4) Write out in Pinyin, with tones, what is written in D1:

C. Miscellaneous Exercises

(1) Circle the person's surname (or family name or **xìng**), and write it in Pinyin romanization, with tones, on the line that follows.

何安南 ________________	安小川 ________________
王明 ________________	都明成 ________________
路廣天 ________________	林京 ________________

(2) Circle the person's first name (or given name or **míngzi**), and write it in Pinyin romanization, with tones, on the line that follows.

王海 ________________	王小文 ________________
李台生 ________________	文大林 ________________
何山 ________________	李京生 ________________

(3) Circle the common component of each character in each group, and write the component on the line that follows.

八六 ________________	十南 ________________
大天 ________________	二五 ________________
川州 ________________	一三 ________________
李林 ________________	港津海 ________________

Reading and Writing Exercises for Lesson B-4

NAME ______________________ COURSE ______________________ DATE ______________________

A. Transcribe what you hear on the accompanying audio disc into Chinese characters.

(1)

(2)

(3)

B. Do as instructed based on the referenced part of this lesson in your textbook.

(1) Write out in Pinyin, with tones, the personal name listed in A5:

(2) Write out in Pinyin, with tones, the place name listed in B6:

(3) Write out in Pinyin, with tones, what is written in C6:

(4) Write out in Pinyin, with tones, what is written in D10:

C. Map Reading Exercise

After each Chinese place name at the bottom of this page, write the corresponding Pinyin, with tones, followed by the place's coordinates on the map (give the coordinates in the form A-1, etc.).

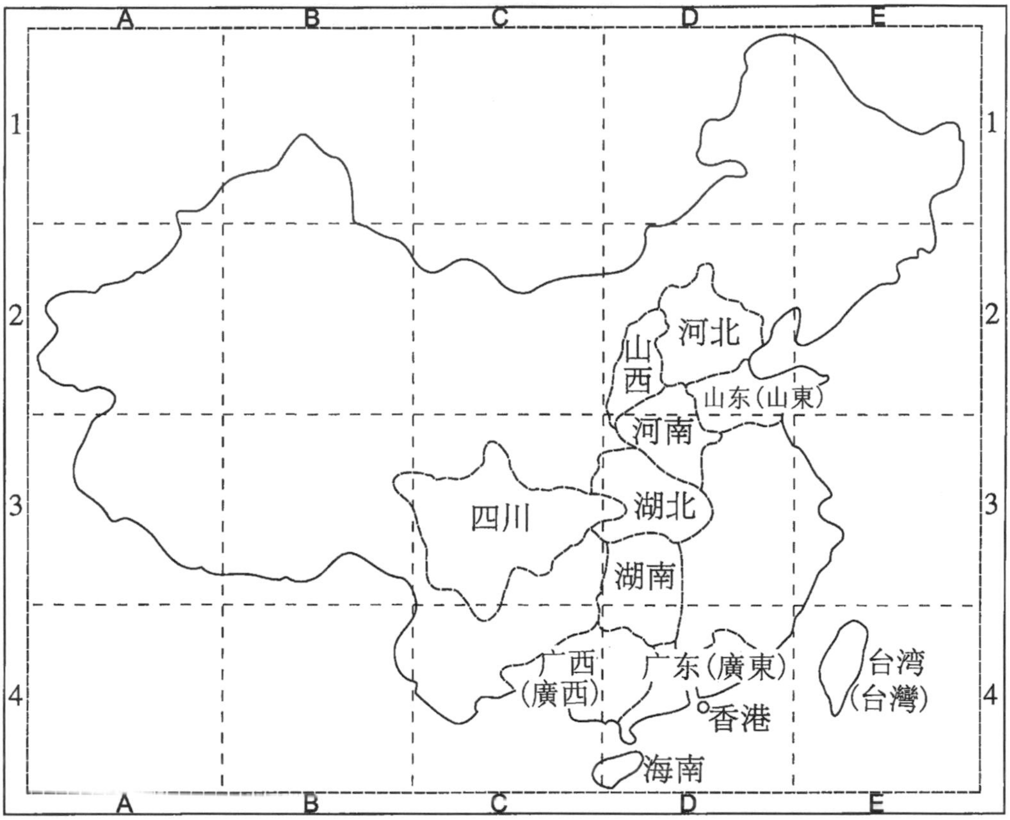

海南 ____________________ 河北 ____________________

河南 ____________________ 湖北 ____________________

湖南 ____________________ 山西 ____________________

四川 ____________________ 香港 ____________________

山东 (山東) ______________ 广东 (廣東) ______________

广西 (廣西) ______________ 台湾 (台灣) ______________

Reading and Writing Exercises for Lesson 1-1

NAME ______________________ COURSE ______________________ DATE ______________________

A. Transcribe what you hear on the accompanying audio disc into Chinese characters.

(1)

(2)

(3)

B. If a reference is given after a question, answer based on the referenced part of the Reading Exercises. If no reference is indicated, you may answer any way you wish

(1) 李小山去河北，王大文呢？ A3

(2) 王安湖去东京。金明呢？(王安湖去東京。金明呢？) D3

(3) 你好！

(4) 我去北京，你呢？

C. Miscellaneous Exercises

Add either 省 or 市 as appropriate to the following geographical terms that you learned in Units A and B.

北京 ________	湖北 ________
台中 ________	成都 ________
河南 ________	台北 ________
山西 ________	上海 ________
海南 ________	湖南 ________
京都 ________	天津 ________
西安 ________	四川 ________
南京 ________	河北 ________
广东 (廣東) ________	东京 (東京) ________
台东 (台東) ________	山东 (山東) ________
广西 (廣西) ________	广州 (廣州) ________

Reading and Writing Exercises for Lesson 1-2

NAME ____________________ COURSE ____________________ DATE ____________________

A. Transcribe what you hear on the accompanying audio disc into Chinese characters.

(1)

(2)

(3)

B. If a reference is given after a question, answer based on the referenced part of the Reading Exercises. If no reference is indicated, you may answer any way you wish.

(1) 王大海去台北吗？(王大海去台北嗎？) A10

(2) 何台生好吗？(何台生好嗎？) B2

(3) 你忙吗？(你忙嗎？)

(4) 你去北京吗？(你去北京嗎？)

C. Miscellaneous Exercises

In the blank in front of each Chinese expression in the left-hand column, write the letter of the best English equivalent from the right-hand column.

________	河北	a. she goes too
________	很忙	b. Sichuan
________	西安	c. avenue
________	你好	d. they
________	四川	e. city of Beijing
________	香港	f. native of Shanghai
________	我去	g. Shanxi Road
________	海南	h. Taiwan
________	大街	i. Hunan Province
________	北京市	j. hello
________	她也去	k. Guangzhou
________	湖南省	l. I go
________	上海人	m. very busy
________	山西路	n. Hainan
________	台湾 (台灣)	o. Xian
________	广州 (廣州)	p. Hebei
________	他们 (他們)	q. Hong Kong

Reading and Writing Exercises for Lesson 1-3

NAME ____________________ COURSE ____________________ DATE ____________________

A. Transcribe what you hear on the accompanying audio disc into Chinese characters.

(1)

(2)

(3)

B. If a reference is given after a question, answer based on the referenced part of the Reading Exercises. If no reference is indicated, you may answer any way you wish.

(1) 林京生也去西安吗？(林京生也去西安嗎？) B3

(2) 台湾人很高吗？(台灣人很高嗎？) D2

(3) 你忙不忙？

(4) 中文难不难？(中文難不難？)

C. Radical Exercise

On each horizontal line under "Character," write one character from *Basic Mandarin Chinese Reading & Writing* A-1 through 1-3 that contains the radical indicated. Also write the Pinyin and basic English meaning of the character. You may consult your textbook as needed.

RADICAL	CHARACTER	PINYIN	ENGLISH
人 or 亻 **rén** "person":	______	______	______
	______	______	______
	______	______	______
水 or 氵 **shuǐ** "water":	______	______	______
	______	______	______
	______	______	______
口 **kǒu** "mouth":	______	______	______
	______	______	______
	______	______	______
女 **nǚ** "woman":	______	______	______
	______	______	______
	______	______	______
木 **mù** "tree":	______	______	______
	______	______	______
	______	______	______
戈 **gē** "spear":	______	______	______
	______	______	______
	______	______	______
大 **dà** "big":	______	______	______
	______	______	______
	______	______	______

Reading and Writing Exercises for Lesson 1-4

NAME ______________________ COURSE ______________________ DATE ______________________

A. Transcribe what you hear on the accompanying audio disc into Chinese characters.

(1)

(2)

(3)

B. If a reference is given after a question, answer based on the referenced part of the Reading Exercises. If no reference is indicated, you may answer any way you wish.

(1) 林小姐忙不忙？ B2

(2) 王太太去不去香港？ D1

(3) 请坐，请坐！(請坐，請坐！)

(4) 我很忙，我先走了。

C. Map Reading Exercise

After each Taiwan place name at the bottom of this page, write the corresponding Pinyin, with tones, followed by the place's coordinates on the map (give the coordinates in the form A-1, etc.).

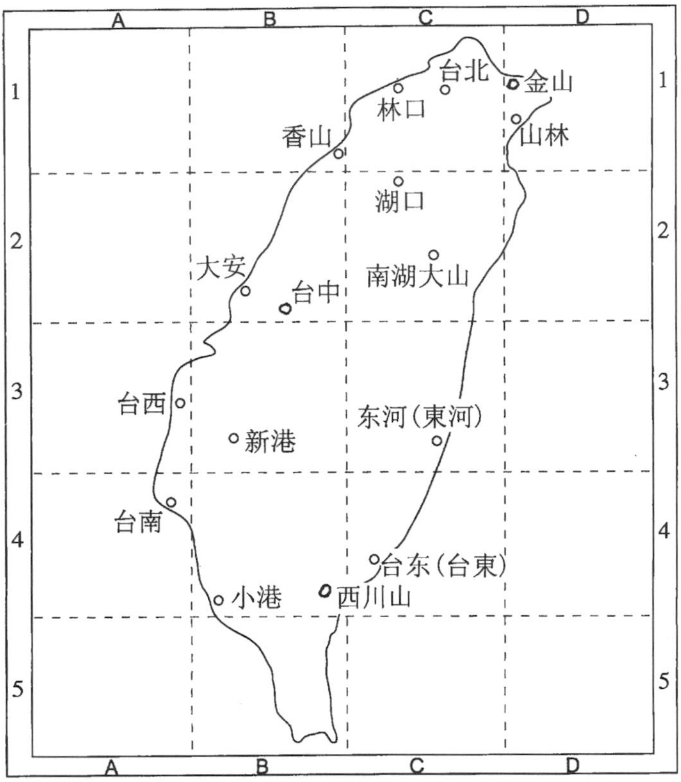

台北 ____________________ 山林 ____________________

香山 ____________________ 台西 ____________________

台南 ____________________ 金山 ____________________

湖口 ____________________ 大安 ____________________

新港 ____________________ 小港 ____________________

台中 ____________________ 林口 ____________________

西川山 ____________________ 南湖大山 ____________________

东河 (東河) ____________________ 台东 (台東) ____________________

Reading and Writing Exercises for Lesson 2-1

NAME ______________________ COURSE ______________________ DATE ______________________

A. Transcribe what you hear on the accompanying audio disc into Chinese characters.

(1)

(2)

(3)

B. If a reference is given after a question, answer based on the referenced part of the Reading Exercises. If no reference is indicated, you may answer any way you wish.

(1) 王大海是美国人吗？(王大海是美國人嗎？) A10

(2) 金小姐、谢小姐、林小姐她们都是中国人吗？(金小姐、謝小姐、林小姐她們都是中國人嗎？) D2

(3) 你是不是叫王明山？

(4) 请问，你是哪国人？(請問，你是哪國人？)

C. Scrambled Sentences

Reorder the following words and phrases to form a sentence, adding punctuation as appropriate.

(1) 了/何/老/何/也/老/太太/先生/了

(2) 人/不都/我们/广东/是 (人/不都/我們/廣東/是)

(3) 小姐/人/是/请问/你/哪国 (小姐/人/是/請問/你/哪國)

(4) 吗/请坐/你/你好/忙/请坐 (嗎/請坐/你/你好/忙/請坐)

(5) 我/我/人/叫/是/林美/美国 (我/我/人/叫/是/林美/美國)

(6) 是/是/我们/我们/你们/你们 (是/是/我們/我們/你們/你們)

(7) 难/难/你/不/忙/忙/中文/不 (難/難/你/不/忙/忙/中文/不)

Reading and Writing Exercises for Lesson 2-2

NAME ______________________ COURSE ______________________ DATE ______________________

A. Transcribe what you hear on the accompanying audio disc into Chinese characters.

(1)

(2)

(3)

B. If a reference is given after a question, answer based on the referenced part of the Reading Exercises. If no reference is indicated, you may answer any way you wish.

(1) 小文是不是小高的同屋？B1

(2) 李小明的同屋是哪国人？(李小明的同屋是哪國人？) D1

(3) 你的名字是不是林美美？

(4) “Doris” 是中国人的名字吗？(「Doris」是中國人的名字嗎？)

C. Miscellaneous Exercises

Use 都 to combine the two shorter sentences into one longer one.

(1) 小林是好人。小安是好人。

(2) 李先生很忙。何先生很忙。

(3) 金太太去北京。路太太去北京。

(4) 我姐姐叫美美。她姐姐叫美美。

(5) 我的同屋叫王大明。你的同屋叫王大明。

(6) 上海很好。广州很好。(上海很好。廣州很好。)

(7) 河北是中国的省。湖北是中国的省。(河北是中國的省。湖北是中國的省。)

Reading and Writing Exercises for Lesson 2-3

NAME ______________________ COURSE ______________________ DATE ______________________

A. Transcribe what you hear on the accompanying audio disc into Chinese characters.

(1)

(2)

(3)

B. If a reference is given after a question, answer based on the referenced part of the Reading Exercises. If no reference is indicated, you may answer any way you wish.

(1) 李文、李同都很高兴吧？(李文、李同都很高興吧？) D1

(2) 谢中文、何台生都不太忙吧？(謝中文、何台生都不太忙吧？) D2

(3) 请问，您贵姓？(請問，您貴姓？)

(4) 我很高兴。你也很高兴吧？(我很高興。你也很高興吧？)

C. Punctuation Exercise

Punctuate each of the following sentences, adding one or more of the Chinese punctuation marks ，、：“”。？！ as appropriate. Then translate each sentence into English.

(1) 高先生李太太何小姐都走了

(2) 老王您别叫我王先生叫我老王好了

(3) 您忙吗中文难不难 (您忙嗎中文難不難)

(4) 我姓谢请问您贵姓 (我姓謝請問您貴姓)

(5) 我很高兴您也高兴吧 (我很高興您也高興吧)

(6) 您好请问您是哪国人 (您好請問您是哪國人)

(7) 他要去广东广西贵州 (他要去廣東廣西貴州)

(8) 她问我你是不是美国人 (她問我你是不是美國人)

Reading and Writing Exercises for Lesson 2-4

NAME ______________________ COURSE ______________________ DATE ______________________

A. Transcribe what you hear on the accompanying audio disc into Chinese characters.

(1)

(2)

(3)

B. If a reference is given after a question, answer based on the referenced part of the Reading Exercises. If no reference is indicated, you may answer any way you wish.

(1) 司先生带名片了吗？(司先生帶名片了嗎？) B1

(2) 这个美国人的中文好不好？(這個美國人的中文好不好？) B2

(3) 请问，你带名片了吗？(請問，你帶名片了嗎？)

(4) 您好！我姓李。这是中美公司的何小姐。(您好！我姓李。這是中美公司的何小姐。)

C. Dialog Completion

Complete the following dialog any way you wish.

A: 你好！

B: ______________________________

A: 我姓王，您贵姓？(我姓王，您貴姓？)

B: ______________________________

A: 我叫王大山，您的名字叫……

B: ______________________________

A: 请问，您是哪国人？(請問，您是哪國人？)

B: ______________________________

A: 中文难不难？(中文難不難？)

B: ______________________________

A: 我先走了，这是我的名片。(我先走了，這是我的名片。)

B: ______________________________

Reading and Writing Exercises for Lesson 3-1

NAME ______________________ COURSE ______________________ DATE ______________________

A. Transcribe what you hear on the accompanying audio disc into Chinese characters.

(1)

(2)

(3)

B. If a reference is given after a question, answer based on the referenced part of the Reading Exercises. If no reference is indicated, you may answer any way you wish.

(1) 他们都是美国人吗？(他們都是美國人嗎？) C4

(2) 高老师是北京人，他的太太也是北京人吧？(高老師是北京人，他的太太也是北京人吧？) E

(3) 美美是男生的名字吗？(美美是男生的名字嗎？)

(4) 你的中文老师都是女的吗？(你的中文老師都是女的嗎？)

C. Same or Different?

Are the following pairs of characters pronounced exactly the SAME, or are their pronunciations DIFFERENT? Put a check mark (√) in the correct box below.

CHARACTERS	SAME	DIFFERENT
十 是		
三 山		
他 她		
京 津		
南 男		
太 台		
四 市		
坐 走		
先 香		
河 何		
街 姐		

CHARACTERS	SAME	DIFFERENT
美 没		
金 京		
名 明		
八 吧		
五 屋		
是 四		
六 路		
何 湖		
津 金		
司 师 (師)		
文 问 (問)		

Reading and Writing Exercises for Lesson 3-2

NAME ______________________ COURSE ______________________ DATE ______________________

A. Transcribe what you hear on the accompanying audio disc into Chinese characters.

(1)

(2)

(3)

B. If a reference is given after a question, answer based on the referenced part of the Reading Exercises. If no reference is indicated, you may answer any way you wish.

(1) 东东今年几岁了？他是哪国人？(東東今年幾歲了？他是哪國人？) E2

(2) 东东的姐姐今年几岁了？她姓安，对不对？(東東的姐姐今年幾歲了？她姓安，對不對？) E2

(3) 你今年多大了？

(4) 中文不太难，对不对？(中文不太難，對不對？)

C. Miscellaneous Exercises

(1) Complete the following numerical sequences by writing in the appropriate Chinese characters.

a) 一，三，五，_____，_____，_____，_____，_____，_____，

_____，_____。

b) 二，四，六，_____，_____，_____，_____，_____，_____，

_____，_____。

c) 十，二十，三十，_____，_____，_____，_____，_____，

_____。

d) 二，三，五，八，_____，_____，_____，_____，_____，

_____，_____，_____。

(2) Translate the Chinese numbers into Arabic numbers and vice versa.

a) 五十三 _____	b) 七十七 _____	c) 九十九 _____
d) 15 _____	e) 94 _____	f) 37 _____
g) 十一 _____	h) 二十九 _____	i) 十八 _____
j) 48 _____	k) 79 _____	l) 88 _____

(3) Transform the following statements into questions by adding a tag question at the end.

她是你姐姐。→

我们(們)去香港。→

中文不太难(難)。→

她八十岁(歲)了。→

这(這)是你的公司。→

Reading and Writing Exercises for Lesson 3-3

NAME ______________________ COURSE ______________________ DATE ______________________

A. Transcribe what you hear on the accompanying audio disc into Chinese characters.

(1)

(2)

(3)

B. If a reference is given after a question, answer based on the referenced part of the Reading Exercises. If no reference is indicated, you may answer any way you wish.

(1) 那位老太太多大年纪了？(那位老太太多大年紀了？) B6

(2) 去天津贵？去上海贵？(去天津貴？去上海貴？) E

(3) 请问，你带了多少钱？(請問，你帶了多少錢？)

(4) 去中国一个人多少钱？(去中國一個人多少錢？)

C. Exercises Involving the Numbers 1-9,999

Translate the following into Chinese characters.

(1) 389

(2) 401

(3) 857

(4) 1,002

(5) 7,652

(6) 9,999

(7) $200.00

(8) $5,589.00

(9) 21 years old

(10) 102 years old

Reading and Writing Exercises for Lesson 3-4

NAME ______________ COURSE ______________ DATE ______________

A. Transcribe what you hear on the accompanying audio disc into Chinese characters.

(1)

(2)

(3)

B. If a reference is given after a question, answer based on the referenced part of the Reading Exercises. If no reference is indicated, you may answer any way you wish.

(1) 那个钟很贵吗？差不多多少钱？(那個鐘很貴嗎？差不多多少錢？) B4

(2) 他们四个人几点去“中美公司”？(他們四個人幾點去「中美公司」？) E

(3) 请问，几点钟了？(請問，幾點鐘了？)

(4) 去中国差不多多少钱？(去中國差不多多少錢？)

C. Clock Times

Write out in Chinese characters the clock times you see indicated on the clock faces.

a) 

b) 

c) 

d) 

e) 

f) 

g) 

h) 

Reading and Writing Exercises for Lesson 4-1

NAME ______________________ COURSE ______________ DATE ______________

A. Transcribe what you hear on the accompanying audio disc into Chinese characters.

(1)

(2)

(3)

B. If a reference is given after a question, answer based on the referenced part of the Reading Exercises. If no reference is indicated, you may answer any way you wish.

(1) 王大海是星期几去中国的？(王大海是星期幾去中國的？) A10

(2) 谁带他们去了台湾？(誰帶他們去了台灣？) D2

(3) 谁是你的中文老师？是王老师吗？(誰是你的中文老師？是王老師嗎？)

(4) 美国的公司星期一几点开门，几点关门？(美國的公司星期一幾點開門，幾點關門？)

C. Radical Exercise

On each horizontal line under "Character," write one character from *Basic Mandarin Chinese Reading & Writing* 1-4 through 3-4 that contains the radical indicated. Also write the Pinyin and basic English meaning of the character. You may consult your textbook as needed.

RADICAL	CHARACTER	PINYIN	ENGLISH
人 or 亻 **rén** "person":	______	______	______
	______	______	______
刀 or 刂 **dāo** "knife":	______	______	______
	______	______	______
口 **kǒu** "mouth":	______	______	______
	______	______	______
	______	______	______
十 **shí** "ten":	______	______	______
	______	______	______
女 **nǚ** "woman":	______	______	______
	______	______	______
土 **tǔ** "earth":	______	______	______
	______	______	______
白 **bái** "white":	______	______	______
	______	______	______
金 **jīn** "gold, metal":	______	______	______
	______	______	______

Reading and Writing Exercises for Lesson 4-2

NAME ____________ COURSE ____________ DATE ____________

A. Transcribe what you hear on the accompanying audio disc into Chinese characters.

(1)

(2)

(3)

B. If a reference is given after a question, answer based on the referenced part of the Reading Exercises. If no reference is indicated, you may answer any way you wish.

(1) 这个中文叫什么？(這個中文叫什麼？) C2

(2) 这个人的先生今年多大年纪了？(這個人的先生今年多大年紀了？) E

(3) 今天是几月几号星期几？(今天是幾月幾號星期幾？)

(4) 你的生日是几月几号？(你的生日是幾月幾號？)

C. Calendar Exercise

Below are four leaves from a typical mainland Chinese desk calendar. Read each leaf and answer the questions below it.

1997年 3月

28

星期五

What is the month, day, and year?

____

What day of the week is it?

____

1997年 10月

15

星期三

What is the month, day and year?

____

What day of the week is it?

____

1997年 6月

5

星期四

Copy the month.

____

Transcribe into Pinyin.

____

1997年 9月

23

星期二

Copy the day of the week.

____

Transcribe into Pinyin.

____

Reading and Writing Exercises for Lesson 4-3

NAME ______________________ COURSE ______________________ DATE ______________________

A. Transcribe what you hear on the accompanying audio disc into Chinese characters.

(1)

(2)

(3)

B. If a reference is given after a question, answer based on the referenced part of the Reading Exercises. If no reference is indicated, you may answer any way you wish.

(1) 那个美国女生要住几天？(那個美國女生要住幾天？) B1

(2) 那个人是几岁第一次去中国的？(那個人是幾歲第一次去中國的？) D

(3) 你去过北京吗？去过几次？(你去過北京嗎？去過幾次？)

(4) 你去过台北吗？去过几次？(你去過台北嗎？去過幾次？)

C. Miscellaneous Exercises

(1) The list below is from a TV guide found in a mainland Chinese hotel room. Read through it and answer in English the questions that follow. (台 means "station.")

电视频道 TV PROGRAM	① 中央 1 台	⑦ 中央 7 台	⑬ 陕西台	⑲ 美国有线电视
	② 中央 2 台	⑧ 中央 8 台	⑭ 江西台	⑳ 德国之声
	③ 中央 3 台	⑨ 湖北台	⑮ 四川台	㉑ 法语音乐台
	④ 中央 4 台	⑩ 湖南台	⑯ 贵州台	㉒ 意大利台
	⑤ 中央 5 台	⑪ 东南台	⑰ 广东台	㉓ 五州法语
	⑥ 中央 6 台	⑫ 山东台	⑱ 湖北1台	㉔ 日文台

a) How many channels are there from Hubei Province?

b) Channel number what is most likely to broadcast in Cantonese?

c) Someone from Sichuan would probably watch channel number what?

d) Someone from Guizhou would probably watch channel number what?

e) A monolingual Japanese would be likely to watch channel number what?

f) A monolingual American would be likely to watch channel number what?

(2) The table below, from a Taipei bank, lists interest rates for CDs for various periods of time. Read the table and answer in English the questions that follow.

一個月	5.00%
三個月	5.35%
五個月	5.50%
六個月	6.00%
七個月	6.00%
九個月	6.15%
一年	6.225%

a) What is the interest rate for three months?

b) What is the interest rate for six months?

c) What is the interest rate for one year?

d) What is the shortest possible term to earn above 6% interest?

e) 5% is the interest rate for what period of time?

Reading and Writing Exercises for Lesson 4-4

NAME ______________________ COURSE ______________________ DATE ______________________

A. Transcribe what you hear on the accompanying audio disc into Chinese characters.

(1)

(2)

(3)

B. If a reference is given after a question, answer based on the referenced part of the Reading Exercises. If no reference is indicated, you may answer any way you wish.

(1) 谁比较高？(誰比較高？) B5

(2) 小李的同屋姓什么？他是哪国人？(小李的同屋姓什麼？他是哪國人？) B8

(3) 请问，你有没有姐姐？(請問，你有沒有姐姐？)

(4) 美国的人口有多少？(美國的人口有多少？)

C. Map Reading Exercise

After each Chinese place name at the bottom of this page, write the corresponding Pinyin, with tones, followed by the place's coordinates on the map (give the coordinates in the form A-1, etc.).

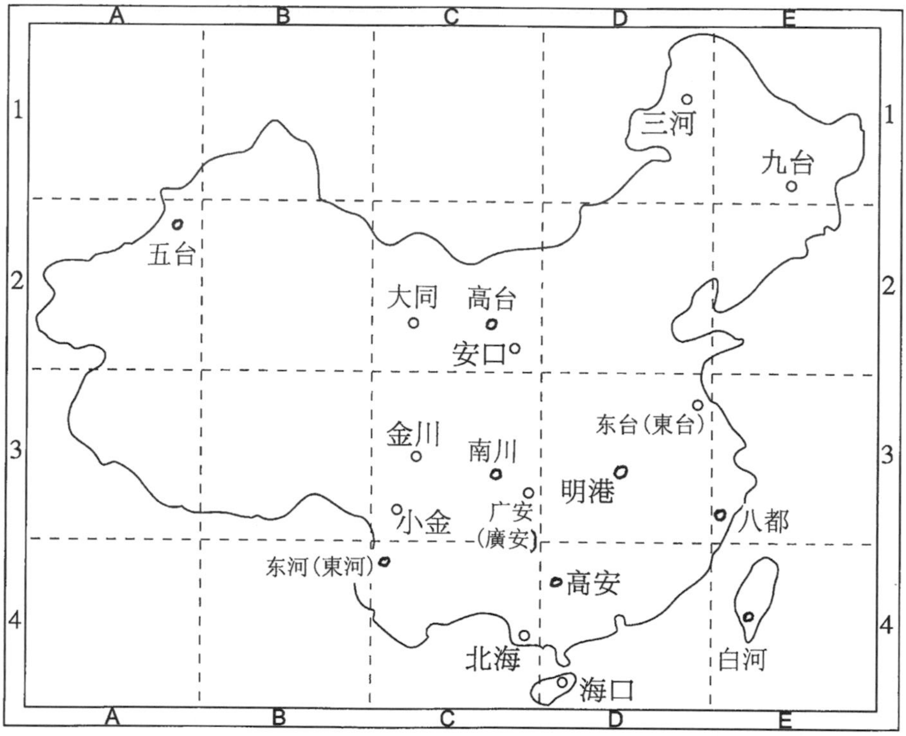

五台 ______________________ 大同 ______________________

白河 ______________________ 小金 ______________________

三河 ______________________ 海口 ______________________

安口 ______________________ 高台 ______________________

金川 ______________________ 明港 ______________________

高安 ______________________ 八都 ______________________

南川 ______________________ 九台 ______________________

北海 ______________________ 广安 (廣安) ______________________

东河 (東河) ______________________ 东台 (東台) ______________________

Reading and Writing Exercises for Lesson 5-1

NAME ______________ COURSE ______________ DATE ______________

A. Transcribe what you hear on the accompanying audio disc into Chinese characters.

(1)

(2)

(3)

B. If a reference is given after a question, answer based on the referenced part of the Reading Exercises. If no reference is indicated, you may answer any way you wish.

(1) 王小姐在吗？(王小姐在嗎？) B2

(2) 万先生知不知道IBM公司的CEO是谁？(萬先生知不知道IBM公司的CEO是誰？) B4

(3) 你姓什么？叫什么名字？(你姓什麼？叫什麼名字？)

(4) 你知不知道中国的人口是多少？(你知不知道中國的人口是多少？)

C. Vocabulary Exercise

There are four words in each row, three of which belong to the same or to a similar semantic or grammatical category. Cross out (with a big "X") the word that has little connection with the other three words in that row.

他	你	她	也
坐	走	钱(錢)	问(問)
大	找	对(對)	高兴(高興)
贵(貴)	好	忙	带(帶)
省	市	门(門)	国(國)
难(難)	老	去	高
可以	知道	同屋	谢谢(謝謝)
六千	六日	六百	六万(六萬)
三月	星期六	五天	四号(四號)
老师(老師)	学生(學生)	大街	上海人
女生	先生	太太	姐姐
金门(金門)	天津	海南	台湾(台灣)
北京	成都	京都	广州(廣州)
人口	海口	海南	河南
台北	台山	台中	台东(台東)
四千	四川	四百	四万(四萬)

Reading and Writing Exercises for Lesson 5-2

NAME ______________________ COURSE ______________________ DATE ______________________

A. Transcribe what you hear on the accompanying audio disc into Chinese characters.

(1)

(2)

(3)

B. If a reference is given after a question, answer based on the referenced part of the Reading Exercises. If no reference is indicated, you may answer any way you wish.

(1) 今年，在美国的大学学中文的学生，男学生多？女学生多？(今年，在美國的大學學中文的學生，男學生多？女學生多？) A9

(2) 香港大学也叫什么？(香港大學也叫什麼？) B2

(3) 你知道北大在哪儿吗？(你知道北大在哪兒嗎？)

(4) 你在哪儿吃中饭？(你在哪兒吃中飯？)

C. China Tour Advertisement

The following was adapted from a newspaper advertisement for a 12-day luxury tour of mainland China for Hong Kong residents. Read the advertisement and answer, in English, the questions that follow. (The advertisement is in traditional characters, but that should not affect your ability to complete this exercise, even if you're studying only simplified characters.)

~ ~ ~ 中國旅遊 ~ ~ ~			
第一天	香港 — 廣州	第七天	西安 — 北京
第二天	廣州 — 海口	第八天	北京
第三天	海口 — 廣州	第九天	北京 — 南京
第四天	廣州 — 成都	第十天	南京 — 上海
第五天	成都 — 西安	第十一天	上海
第六天	西安	第十二天	上海 — 香港

(1) What is the destination on the second day?

(2) What is the destination on the fourth day?

(3) Where will the tour members be on the sixth day?

(4) Does the tour include Tianjin? If so, on which day?

(5) Does the tour include Nanjing? If so, on which day?

(6) Where will the tour be headed on the tenth day?

(7) In what city does the tour end?

(8) Which city will the tour members arrive in twice?

(9) Not including that city, in which cities will the tour members spend an entire day or longer?

(10) Not including Hong Kong, what is the total number of different cities the tour members will visit?

Reading and Writing Exercises for Lesson 5-3

NAME ______________________ COURSE ______________________ DATE ______________________

A. Transcribe what you hear on the accompanying audio disc into Chinese characters.

(1)

(2)

(3)

B. If a reference is given after a question, answer based on the referenced part of the Reading Exercises. If no reference is indicated, you may answer any way you wish.

(1) 海南省在什么地方？(海南省在什麼地方？) A7

(2) 王大海知道什么？(王大海知道什麼？) A10

(3) 你住在什么地方？(你住在什麼地方？)

(4) 你都住过什么饭店？(你都住過什么飯店？)

C. Reading a Table

The table below, compiled by the Hong Kong Hospital Authority and copied here verbatim, shows the number of new cases of H1N1 virus (also known as swine flu) in Hong Kong during part of winter 2011. Read the first three columns of the table and answer in English the questions that follow. (Since the table appeared in Hong Kong, it's in traditional characters, but in the first three columns of the table, which is all you need to read to answer the questions, there are only two traditional characters that would be different in simplified script: 歲=岁 and 個=个.)

近日H1N1甲型流感個案#:			
2月11日	男	56歲	嚴重
2月9日	男	7歲	危殆
2月9日	男	39歲	危殆
2月8日	女	45歲	危殆
2月7日	女	16歲	危殆
2月6日	男	53歲	死亡
2月5日	女	23個月	危殆
2月4日	女	21歲	死亡

#資料來源：香港醫院管理局新聞稿（2011年2月5 - 11日）

(1) What is the time period covered by this table?

(2) What was the total number of patients during this period?

(3) How many male patients were there and how many female patients?

(4) How old was the oldest male patient?

(5) How old was the oldest female patient?

(6) How old was the youngest patient?

(7) Describe the patient who entered the hospital on February 7?

(8) Describe the patients who entered the hospital on February 9?

Reading and Writing Exercises for Lesson 5-4

NAME ______________________ COURSE ______________ DATE ______________

A. Transcribe what you hear on the accompanying audio disc into Chinese characters.

(1)

(2)

(3)

B. If a reference is given after a question, answer based on the referenced part of the Reading Exercises. If no reference is indicated, you may answer any way you wish.

(1) 那个人的名片在哪儿？(那個人的名片在哪兒？) A6

(2) 中大里边的饭店比较贵，对不对？(中大裡邊的飯店比較貴，對不對？) D

(3) 你下个月要去哪儿？(你下個月要去哪兒？)

(4) 你的中文太好了！

C. Writing a Dialog

In the space below, make up a dialog. You can have the speakers in your dialog say anything you wish. The only requirements are: (1) each speaker should say at least 4 lines; and (2) you should use at least 12 of the 24 new characters in Unit 5 in your dialog (please underline the new characters).

Reading and Writing Exercises for Lesson 6-1

NAME ______________________ COURSE ______________ DATE ______________

A. Transcribe what you hear on the accompanying audio disc into Chinese characters.

(1)

(2)

(3)

B. If a reference is given after a question, answer based on the referenced part of the Reading Exercises. If no reference is indicated, you may answer any way you wish.

(1) 这个人喜欢北京，不过他的朋友比较喜欢什么地方？(這個人喜歡北京，不過他的朋友比較喜歡什麼地方？) A1

(2) 什么叫"好朋友"？(什麼叫「好朋友」？) D1

(3) 你喜欢中文吗？(你喜歡中文嗎？)

(4) 你有没有中国朋友？(你有沒有中國朋友？)

C. Answer the following questions using 过 (過).

(1) 你上过高中吗？(你上過高中嗎？)

(2) 你学过中文吗？(你學過中文嗎？)

(3) 你去过海南省吗？(你去過海南省嗎？)

(4) 你在“北京饭店”吃过饭吗？(你在「北京飯店」吃過飯嗎？)

D. Use 可是 to combine the two short sentences into one longer one.

(1) 小安是我的好朋友。他不是我的男朋友。

(2) 我喜欢中文。中文很难学。(我喜歡中文。中文很難學。)

(3) 小李喜欢小王。小王不喜欢小李。(小李喜歡小王。小王不喜歡小李。)

(4) 老何请我吃饭。我有事儿，不能去。(老何請我吃飯。我有事兒，不能去。)

Reading and Writing Exercises for Lesson 6-2

NAME ______________________ COURSE ______________________ DATE ______________________

A. Transcribe what you hear on the accompanying audio disc into Chinese characters.

(1)

(2)

(3)

B. If a reference is given after a question, answer based on the referenced part of the Reading Exercises. If no reference is indicated, you may answer any way you wish.

(1) 那个中国人是哪里人？(那個中國人是哪裡人？) B1

(2) 林东生一天学几个钟头的中文？你呢？(林東生一天學幾個鐘頭的中文？你呢？) D

(3) 你还没有三十岁吧？(你還沒有三十歲吧？)

(4) 你是在哪里出生，在哪里长大的？(你是在哪裡出生，在哪裡長大的？)

C. Transforming Statements into Questions

Write questions for the answers below. Note that the underlined portion is stressed and is what you should be asking about.

(1) 今天是<u>星期五</u>。

(2) 高小姐要去<u>上海</u>。

(3) 小李的男朋友叫<u>方大中</u>。

(4) 明天是<u>十月一号</u>。(明天是<u>十月一號</u>。)

(5) 何先生是<u>中国人</u>。(何先生是<u>中國人</u>。)

(6) 那个钟要<u>两千块钱</u>!(那個鐘要<u>兩千塊錢</u>!)

(7) 我们的中文老师是<u>左老师</u>。(我們的中文老師是<u>左老師</u>。)

Reading and Writing Exercises for Lesson 6-3

NAME ______________________ COURSE ______________________ DATE ______________________

A. Transcribe what you hear on the accompanying audio disc into Chinese characters.

(1)

(2)

(3)

B. If a reference is given after a question, answer based on the referenced part of the Reading Exercises. If no reference is indicated, you may answer any way you wish.

(1) 为什么安老师、司老师要走了？(為什麼安老師、司老師要走了？) B2

(2) 为什么李大海的中国朋友叫他“半个广州人”？(為什麼李大海的中國朋友叫他「半個廣州人」？) D

(3) 你为什么要学中文？(你為什麼要學中文？)

(4) 你工作过没有？在哪儿？(你工作過沒有？在哪兒？)

C. Work Schedule Exercise

Below is the first draft of a schedule for employees of the Commercial Section of US Embassy Beijing to assist American exporters at a trade fair. Per request of the Ambassador, there should be two Americans and two local Chinese employees of the Embassy on duty each day (Chang and those with the Western names are American, all others are Chinese). Read the schedule and answer the questions in Chinese.

MAY 2 (MON.)	MAY 3 (TUES.)	MAY 4 (WED.)	MAY 5 (THURS.)	MAY 6 (FRI.)	MAY 7 (SAT.)
Parker	Parker	Qian	Gonzales		Wan
Chang	Wan	Gonzales	Donovan		Li
Li	Donovan		Chang		
Wang	Qian				
	Wang				

(1) 五月二号有几个人工作？(五月二號有幾個人工作？)

(2) 哪一天人太多？

(3) 哪一天还没有人工作？(哪一天還沒有人工作？)

(4) 星期六还要多找几个人？(星期六還要多找幾個人？)

(5) 哪一天中国人太多？(哪一天中國人太多？)

(6) 哪三天美国人太少？(哪三天美國人太少？)

Reading and Writing Exercises for Lesson 6-4

NAME ______________________ COURSE ______________ DATE ______________

A. Transcribe what you hear on the accompanying audio disc into Chinese characters.

(1)

(2)

(3)

B. If a reference is given after a question, answer based on the referenced part of the Reading Exercises. If no reference is indicated, you may answer any way you wish.

(1) 王大海在他们家是老几？(王大海在他們家是老幾？) A10

(2) 高明山的老师为什么不太喜欢他？(高明山的老師為什麼不太喜歡他？) D

(3) 要是有人给你他的名片，你也给他你的名片吗？(要是有人給你他的名片，你也給他你的名片嗎？)

(4) 要是有人给你他的名片，可是你忘了带你的名片，你说什么？(要是有人給你他的名片，可是你忘了帶你的名片，你說什麼？)

C. Miscellaneous Exercises

Answer the following questions about your family.

(1) 你们家里有几个人？(你們家裡有幾個人？)

(2) 你有哥哥吗？(你有哥哥嗎？)

(3) 你有没有姐姐？(你有沒有姐姐？)

(4) 你有几个弟弟？(你有幾個弟弟？)

(5) 你有几个妹妹？(你有幾個妹妹？)

(6) 你有儿子、女儿吗？(你有兒子、女兒嗎？)

Reading and Writing Exercises for Lesson 7-1

NAME ______________________ COURSE ______________________ DATE ______________________

A. Transcribe what you hear on the accompanying audio disc into Chinese characters.

(1)

(2)

(3)

B. If a reference is given after a question, answer based on the referenced part of the Reading Exercises. If no reference is indicated, you may answer any way you wish.

(1) 高先生家里有几口人？他有没有儿子、女儿？(高先生家裡有幾口人？他有沒有兒子、女兒？) D

(2) 高先生为什么开了这家工厂？(高先生為什麼開了這家工廠？) D

(3) 你有没有表哥、表姐、表弟、表妹？(你有沒有表哥、表姐、表弟、表妹？)

(4) 现在几点？(現在幾點？)

C. Radical Exercise

On each horizontal line under "Character," write one character from *Basic Mandarin Chinese Reading & Writing* 4-1 through 6-4 that contains the radical indicated. Also write the Pinyin and basic English meaning of the character. You may consult your textbook as needed.

RADICAL	CHARACTER	PINYIN	ENGLISH
目 **mù** "eye":	________	________	________
	________	________	________
车(車) **chē** "vehicle":	________	________	________
	________	________	________
月 **yuè** "moon":	________	________	________
	________	________	________
	________	________	________
土 **tǔ** "earth":	________	________	________
	________	________	________
日 **rì** "sun":	________	________	________
	________	________	________
囗 **wéi** "enclose":	________	________	________
	________	________	________
辶 **chuò** "walk, go":	________	________	________
	________	________	________
纟(糸) **sī** "silk":	________	________	________
	________	________	________

Reading and Writing Exercises for Lesson 7-2

NAME ______________________ COURSE ______________ DATE ______________

A. Transcribe what you hear on the accompanying audio disc into Chinese characters.

(1)

(2)

(3)

B. If a reference is given after a question, answer based on the referenced part of the Reading Exercises. If no reference is indicated, you may answer any way you wish.

(1) 这个人的朋友都是男的，对不对？(這個人的朋友都是男的，對不對？) A5

(2) 林老太太的女儿会说什么地方的话？(林老太太的女兒會說什麼地方的話？) D

(3) 你会不会说中国话？(你會不會說中國話？)

(4) 你会写多少个中国字？(你會寫多少個中國字？)

C. Exercise on Characters with Multiple Pronunciations

Read each sentence and, paying careful attention to the context and meaning, decide what the correct pronunciation of the bolded character is. Write the Pinyin for that character in the blank after the sentence, and write an English translation of the whole sentence underneath it.

(1) 我星期一要去成**都**了。[都: _____]

(2) 我表哥、表姐**都**在那家公司工作。[都: _____]

(3) 你得学**得**好一点。(你得學**得**好一點。) [得: _____]

(4) 我**得**回家了，先走了。[得: _____]

(5) 你中国话说**得**太好了！(你中國話說**得**太好了！) [得: _____]

(6) 你儿子**长**高了！(你兒子**長**高了！) [长(長): _____]

(7) 你女儿**长**得很好看。(你女兒**長**得很好看。) [长(長): _____]

(8) 我还得走很**长**的路。(我還得走很**長**的路。) [长(長): _____]

(9) 她是在哪儿**长**大的？(她是在哪兒**長**大的？) [长(長): _____]

(10) 他的名字可真**长**！(他的名字可真**長**！) [长(長): _____]

Reading and Writing Exercises for Lesson 7-3

NAME ______________________ COURSE ______________________ DATE ______________________

A. Transcribe what you hear on the accompanying audio disc into Chinese characters.

(1)

(2)

(3)

B. If a reference is given after a question, answer based on the referenced part of the Reading Exercises. If no reference is indicated, you may answer any way you wish.

(1) 那个美国人下个月又要到什么地方去？(那個美國人下個月又要到什麼地方去？) B2

(2) 李老先生是一个人到台湾去的吗？(李老先生是一個人到台灣去的嗎？) D2

(3) 你是在哪儿学的中文？(你是在哪兒學的中文？)

(4) 你的中文是什么时候开始学的？(你的中文是什麼時候開始學的？)

C. Travel Notes

Many Chinese tourists now visit Taiwan, which was not possible until recently. Below are notes from the calendar of Mrs. Guan, an elderly mainland tourist who, together with her husband, just made her first trip to Taiwan. Read her calendar and answer in Chinese the questions that follow.

七月

14 星期一	到台北
15 星期二	去台中
16 星期三	去台南
17 星期四	去台东
18 星期五	回台北
19 星期六	去金门
20 星期日	回台北

(1) 关老太太是几月几号星期几到台湾的？(關老太太是幾月幾號星期幾到台灣的？)

(2) 她第一天住在什么地方？(她第一天住在什麼地方？)

(3) 第二天她去了哪儿？(第二天她去了哪兒？)

(4) 星期四她住在哪里？(星期四她住在哪裏？)

(5) 关老太太星期五回台北，什么时候又回台北了？(關老太太星期五回台北，什麼時候又回台北了？)

(6) 她是几月几号去的金门？(她是幾月幾號去的金門？)

(7) 关老太太是一个人到台湾去的吗？(關老太太是一個人到台灣去的嗎？)

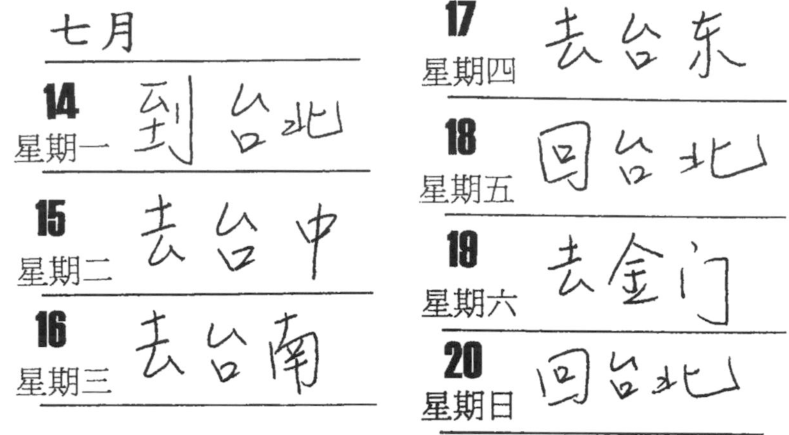

Reading and Writing Exercises for Lesson 7-4

NAME ______________________ COURSE ______________ DATE ______________

A. Transcribe what you hear on the accompanying audio disc into Chinese characters.

(1)

(2)

(3)

B. If a reference is given after a question, answer based on the referenced part of the Reading Exercises. If no reference is indicated, you may answer any way you wish.

(1) 王大海的中国字写得好不好看？(王大海的中國字寫得好不好看？) A10

(2) 来美国之前，这个中国人在哪里工作？(來美國之前，這個中國人在哪裡工作？) B1

(3) 你知不知道你的中文老师是从哪儿来的？中国？台湾？香港？(你知不知道你的中文老師是從哪兒來的？中國？台灣？香港？)

(4) 你以后要在哪儿工作？中国？美国？(你以後要在哪兒工作？中國？美國？)

C. Map Reading Exercise

After each place name at the bottom of this page, write the Pinyin followed by the place's coordinates on the map. Note that the character 兴 (興), which you learned with the pronunciation **xìng** as in 高兴 (高興) **gāoxìng**, is pronounced **xīng** when it occurs in geographical names.

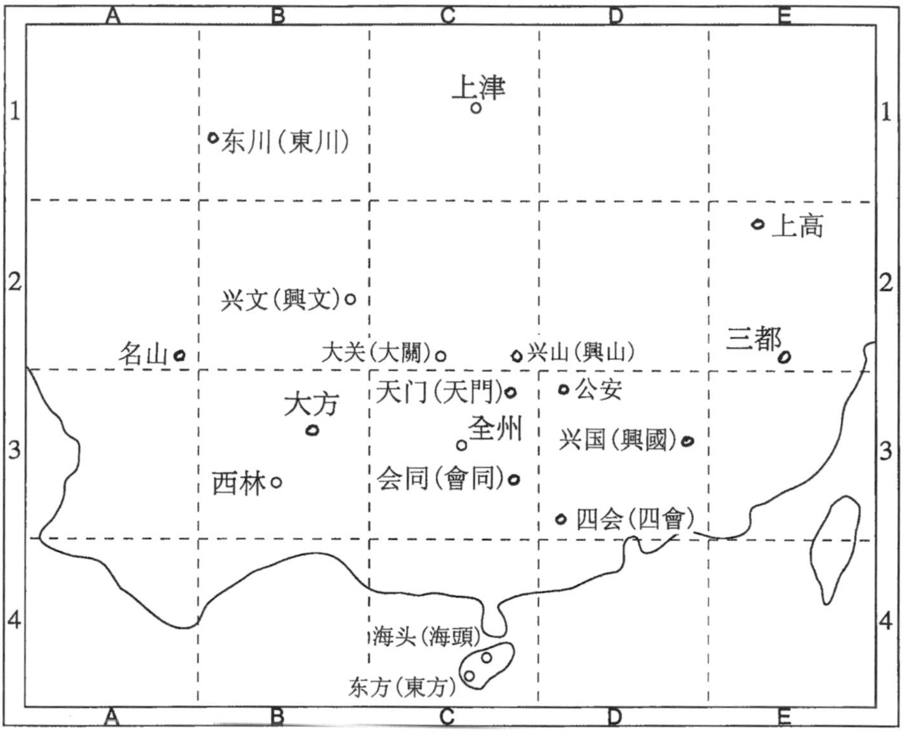

全州 ______________________ 上津 ______________________

上高 ______________________ 三都 ______________________

西林 ______________________ 公安 ______________________

名山 ______________________ 大方 ______________________

兴山 (興山) ______________________ 兴国 (興國) ______________________

东川 (東川) ______________________ 东方 (東方) ______________________

会同 (會同) ______________________ 兴文 (興文) ______________________

大关 (大關) ______________________ 天门 (天門) ______________________

四会 (四會) ______________________ 海头 (海頭) ______________________

Reading and Writing Exercises for Lesson 8-1

NAME ______________________ COURSE ______________________ DATE ______________________

A. Transcribe what you hear on the accompanying audio disc into Chinese characters.

(1)

(2)

(3)

B. If a reference is given after a question, answer based on the referenced part of the Reading Exercises. If no reference is indicated, you may answer any way you wish.

(1) 那个小姐怎么知道那个先生是北方人？(那個小姐怎麼知道那個先生是北方人？) B3

(2) 钱老先生先说去天安门得怎么走？(錢老先生先說去天安門得怎麼走？) D1

(3) 你住的地方离你学中文的地方远不远？(你住的地方離你學中文的地方遠不遠？)

(4) 你的中国话说得太好了！(你的中國話說得太好了！)

C. Choose the Right Homonym!

Many characters are homonyms, i.e., have the same pronunciation but different meanings. Even native writers sometimes mix them up, especially when writing via computer. From the choices given in brackets after each sentence below, choose the right homonym and write it in the blank.

(1) 那位是中美 ____ 司的方小姐。[工 公]

(2) 王先生和他太太都是 ____ 方人。[男 南 难(難)]

(3) 这是他 ____ 二次去中国。(這是他 ____ 二次去中國。) [地 弟 第]

(4) 我们 ____ 你们一起去吧。(我們 ____ 你們一起去吧。) [何 河 和]

(5) 你觉 ____ 中国字很难写吗？(你覺 ____ 中國字很難寫嗎？)
[的 得]

(6) 开关在 ____ 边，不在左边。(開關在 ____ 邊，不在左邊。)
[又 右]

(7) 你的中国话说 ____ 太好了！(你的中國話說 ____ 太好了！)
[的 得]

(8) 对不起，我今天没带 ____ 片。(對不起，我今天沒帶 ____ 片。)
[名 明]

(9) 我很高 ____ 能来这儿学中文。(我很高 ____ 能來這兒學中文。)
[姓 兴(興)]

(10) 从北京到长城要几个 ____ 头？(從北京到長城要幾個 ____ 頭？)
[中 钟(鐘)]

(11) 住北京饭店一天得多少 ____？(住北京飯店一天得多少 ____？)
[前 钱(錢)]

Reading and Writing Exercises for Lesson 8-2

NAME ______________________ COURSE ______________ DATE ______________

A. Transcribe what you hear on the accompanying audio disc into Chinese characters.

(1)

(2)

(3)

B. If a reference is given after a question, answer based on the referenced part of the Reading Exercises. If no reference is indicated, you may answer any way you wish.

(1) 汽车公司的人要那个外国人在哪里等车？(汽車公司的人要那個外國人在哪裡等車？) B1

(2) 王先生的家离首都机场远吗？(王先生的家離首都機場遠嗎？) D2

(3) 你有没有汽车？(你有沒有汽車？)

(4) 你都会说什么外国话？(你都會說什麼外國話？)

C. Word Study

(1) Use each character printed below to create three two-syllable words that all share the same first syllable. The first item is done for you as an example.

大	同	好	高
概 哥 街	__________	__________	__________
北	表	外	上
__________	__________	__________	__________
小	后(後)	开(開)	里(裏)
__________	__________	__________	__________

(2) Now, use each character printed below to create three two-syllable words that all share the same last syllable. Again, the first item is done for you as an example.

前 上 外	__________	__________	__________
面	口	子	月
__________	__________	__________	__________
年	前	西	国(國)
__________	__________	__________	__________
边(邊)	里(裏)	头(頭)	后(後)
__________	__________	__________	__________

(3) Write in Chinese characters an antonym of the word given.

大 ________	多 ________	左 ________	去 ________
近 ________	前面 ________	上面 ________	外面 ________
女生 ________	开(開) ________	老 ________	

Reading and Writing Exercises for Lesson 8-3

NAME ______________________ COURSE ______________ DATE ______________

A. Transcribe what you hear on the accompanying audio disc into Chinese characters.

(1)

(2)

(3)

B. If a reference is given after a question, answer based on the referenced part of the Reading Exercises. If no reference is indicated, you may answer any way you wish.

(1) 班先生很不喜欢在什么时候开车？为什么？(班先生很不喜歡在什麼時候開車？為什麼？) D

(2) 班先生一天得工作几个小时？(班先生一天得工作幾個小時？) D

(3) 美国的公司大概几点钟上班，几点钟下班？(美國的公司大概幾點鐘上班，幾點鐘下班？)

(4) 要是你半小时以前打过电话要车，可是车子到现在还没来，那么你第二次打电话要怎么说？(要是你半小時以前打過電話要車，可是車子到現在還沒來，那麼你第二次打電話要怎麼說？)

C. Name Card Reading Exercise

For each name card, you should: (1) circle the person's surname and write it in Pinyin next to the character; (2) circle the city where the person lives and write it in Pinyin next to the characters; (3) find the telephone number and circle it. Try to read as much of the rest of the name card as you can.

中央研究院 院長
李遠哲
地址：台北市南港區研究院路二段
電話：（〇二）七八九—[redacted]〇〇
傳真：（〇二）七八五—[redacted]五二
電子郵件：[redacted]@gate.sinica.edu.tw

國立台灣師範大學
英語系副教授
謝國平
住址：台北縣新店市百忍街[redacted]巷6號五樓
電話：九一四[redacted]二五

國立台灣大學
國際華語研習所
柏克萊・台大商業中文課程執行主任
林雪芳
ICLP
通訊地址：台北市 106 大安區
郵政十三之二〇四號信箱
電話：(〇二)二三[redacted]—九一二三
傳真：(〇二)二三[redacted]—六九二六
電子郵件：[redacted]@ms13.hinet.net

北京北方出租汽车公司
王建新
手机: 13[redacted]1101964
车型: 爱丽舍
车号: 京 B-J9220
长短途包车
Long and short car rental
优惠号: 盛 3819
机场接送 长城十三陵观光
Airport pick-up drop-off the great wall ming tomb tour city tour

中央研究院
語言學研究所
研究員兼所長
何大安
11529 台北市 南港區 研究院路二段[redacted]號
電話：+886-2-26[redacted]-5013
傳真：+886-2-26[redacted]-6622
電子郵件：[redacted]@gate.sinica.edu.tw
網址：http://www.[redacted].sinica.edu.tw

中山大學 心理学系
高定国 副教授
系主任
脑功能影像研究中心副主任
地址：广州市中山大学心理学系
邮政编码：510275
Email:[redacted]@zsu.edu.cn
电话：020-84[redacted]4268
传真：020-84[redacted]4266

復旦大學
副校长
金力 博士、教授
FUDAN UNIVERSITY 1905
中国上海
邯郸路[redacted]号
邮政编码: 200433
电话: 0086-21-65[redacted]1600
传真: 0086-21-65[redacted]4937
E-mail: [redacted]@fudan.edu.cn

Reading and Writing Exercises for Lesson 8-4

NAME ____________ COURSE ____________ DATE ____________

A. Transcribe what you hear on the accompanying audio disc into Chinese characters.

(1)

(2)

(3)

B. If a reference is given after a question, answer based on the referenced part of the Reading Exercises. If no reference is indicated, you may answer any way you wish.

(1) 那个人为什么说“我们只好换别的路走了”？(那個人為什麼說「我們只好換別的路走了」？) A7

(2) 那个美国学生说从他家到北京需要多长时间？(那個美國學生說從他家到北京需要多長時間？) D3

(3) 要是你到中国去的话，会带几件行李？(要是你到中國去的話，會帶幾件行李？)

(4) 你会不会开车？要是会的话，你是什么时候学的？(你會不會開車？要是會的話，你是什麼時候學的？)

C. Name Card Drafting Exercise

(1) You have an American friend in Hong Kong who doesn't know Chinese but would like to have some name cards printed. In the space below, draw a rectangle, then draft the Chinese side of the name card for her, being sure to include all of the following information in Chinese characters:

Organization: Sino-American Transportation Company
Person's name in Chinese: 林文美
Telephone number: 2948 7174
Address: No. 10, Canton (Guangzhou) Road,
Hong Kong

In drafting the name card, you may wish to refer to the name cards in *Basic Mandarin Chinese Reading & Writing* 8-3 and page182 of this practice book for guidance. You may write either horizontally or vertically.

(2) Now create a name card of your own! Again, consider this a draft to be given to a print shop. As a minimum, include your Chinese name, your telephone number, and an imaginary address in some city in a Chinese-speaking region where you might like to live. Add other information if you wish. You may write either horizontally or vertically.

Reading and Writing Exercises for Lesson 9-1

NAME ______________________ COURSE ______________ DATE ______________

A. Transcribe what you hear on the accompanying audio disc into Chinese characters.

(1)

(2)

(3)

B. If a reference is given after a question, answer based on the referenced part of the Reading Exercises. If no reference is indicated, you may answer any way you wish.

(1) 从1928年一直到1949年，“北京”叫什么？(從1928年一直到1949年，「北京」叫什麼？) A2

(2) 到和平饭店差不多要走几分钟？(到和平飯店差不多要走幾分鐘？) B1

(3) 你会不会说日本话？(你會不會說日本話？)

(4) 你的学校有多少人学中文，你清楚不清楚？(你的學校有多少人學中文，你清楚不清楚？)

C. Phonetic Exercise

The characters below, all of which have been introduced somewhere in *Basic Mandarin Chinese Reading & Writing* A-1 through 9-1, have been arranged into a number of different phonetic groups so that each member of a group shares the same phonetic with the other members of that group. Do the following: (1) circle the phonetic in each character; and (2) under each character write its pronunciation in Pinyin with tone.

又友

子字

忙忘

那哪

弟第

成城

生姓星

可哥何河

几机 (幾機)

清请 (清請)

点店 (點店)

交校较 (交校較)

门们问 (門們問)

Reading and Writing Exercises for Lesson 9-2

NAME ______________ COURSE ______________ DATE ______________

A. Transcribe what you hear on the accompanying audio disc into Chinese characters.

(1)

(2)

(3)

B. If a reference is given after a question, answer based on the referenced part of the Reading Exercises. If no reference is indicated, you may answer any way you wish.

(1) 他们先去哪儿？然后去哪儿？(他們先去哪兒？然後去哪兒？) A2

(2) 我要从北京南站到动物园，得坐几路车？(我要從北京南站到動物園，得坐幾路車？) E

(3) 你喜欢不喜欢去动物园？(你喜歡不喜歡去動物園？)

(4) 你住的地方有没有公共汽车可以到？(你住的地方有沒有公共汽車可以到？)

C. Radical Exercise

On each horizontal line under "Character," write one character from *Basic Mandarin Chinese Reading & Writing* 7-1 through 9-2 that contains the radical indicated. Also write the Pinyin and basic English meaning of the character. You may consult your textbook as needed.

RADICAL	CHARACTER	PINYIN	ENGLISH
手 or 扌 **shǒu** "hand":	________	________	________
	________	________	________
水 or 氵 **shuǐ** "water ":	________	________	________
	________	________	________
刀 or 刂 **dāo** "knife":	________	________	________
	________	________	________
土 **tǔ** "earth":	________	________	________
	________	________	________
彳 **chì** "short slow step":	________	________	________
	________	________	________
讠(言) **yán** "speech":	________	________	________
	________	________	________
玉 **yù** "jade":	________	________	________
	________	________	________
辶 **chuò** "walk, go":	________	________	________
	________	________	________

Reading and Writing Exercises for Lesson 9-3

NAME ______________________ COURSE ______________________ DATE ______________________

A. Transcribe what you hear on the accompanying audio disc into Chinese characters.

(1)

(2)

(3)

B. If a reference is given after a question, answer based on the referenced part of the Reading Exercises. If no reference is indicated, you may answer any way you wish.

(1) 那个外国人是什么时候上的公车？(那個外國人是什麼時候上的公車？) B1

(2) 为什么那个人以后不给她的表姐买票了？(為什麼那個人以後不給她的表姐買票了？) D1

(3) 在美国，一张公车票卖多少钱？(在美國，一張公車票賣多少錢？)

(4) 要是有人给你一百块钱的话，你会买什么东西？(要是有人給你一百塊錢的話，你會買什麼東西？)

C. Measure Exercise

Write in the appropriate measure word.

(1) 一 ____ 人

(2) 一 ____ 行李

(3) 三 ____ "three days"

(4) 哪 ____ ？ "which year?"

(5) 三 ____ 人 [don't use 个(個)]

(6) 两 ____ 票 (兩 ____ 票)

(7) 这 ____ 路 (這 ____ 路)

(8) 那 ____ 名片

(9) 这 ____ (這 ____) "this time"

(10) 第一 ____ "the first time" [don't use 次]

(11) 一 ____ 钱 (一 ____ 錢) "a dime"

(12) 一 ____ 钟 (一 ____ 鐘) "1 minute"

(13) 一 ____ 钱 (一 ____ 錢) "one dollar"

(14) 一 ____ 钟 (一 ____ 鐘) "15 minutes"

(15) 一 ____ 钟 (一 ____ 鐘) "one o'clock"

(16) 这 ____ 老师 (這 ____ 老師) [be polite]

(17) 一 ____ 钟头 (一 ____ 鐘頭) "one hour"

(18) 二十一 ____ [years of age]

(19) 这 ____ 公司 (這 ____ 公司) [don't use 个(個)]

(20) 几 ____ ？(幾 ____ ？) "which day of the month?"

(21) 这 ____ (這 ____) [when talking about computers]

(22) 几 ____ 车？(幾 ____ 車？) "what bus number?"

Reading and Writing Exercises for Lesson 9-4

NAME ______________________ COURSE ______________________ DATE ______________________

A. Transcribe what you hear on the accompanying audio disc into Chinese characters.

(1)

(2)

(3)

B. If a reference is given after a question, answer based on the referenced part of the Reading Exercises. If no reference is indicated, you may answer any way you wish.

(1) 你要不要大海给你准备早饭？为什么？(你要不要大海給你準備早飯？為什麼？) A10

(2) 那个外国人找不着他的车票，公车小姐说什么？(那個外國人找不着他的車票，公車小姐說什麼？) B1

(3) 你早上吃不吃早饭？(你早上吃不吃早飯？)

(4) 请问，你准备以后到中国去工作吗？(請問，你準備以後到中國去工作嗎？)

C. Bus Advertisement

Read the advertisement on the side of this Taipei bus:

HINTS: 永庆 (永慶) **Yǒngqìng** is a person's name. 房屋 **fángwū** means "houses, homes." Also, note that the verb-object compound 下車 is written as 下车 in simplified characters.

(1) Transcribe the whole advertisement into Pinyin.

____

(2) Write down below an English translation of the advertisement.

____

(3) Now, answer the following questions in Chinese.

"我" 在哪儿下车？(「我」在哪兒下車？)

____

"我" 问 "你" 什么？(「我」問「你」什麼？)

____

"我" 要 "你" 到哪儿去？为什么？(「我」要「你」到哪兒去？為什麼？)

____

Reading and Writing Exercises for Lesson 10-1

NAME ______________________ COURSE ______________________ DATE ______________________

A. Transcribe what you hear on the accompanying audio disc into Chinese characters.

(1)

(2)

(3)

B. If a reference is given after a question, answer based on the referenced part of the Reading Exercises. If no reference is indicated, you may answer any way you wish.

(1) 为什么李先生觉得王先生可能得换工作？(為什麼李先生覺得王先生可能得換工作？) B1

(2) 最近在中国，几个字的姓名越来越多？(最近在中國，幾個字的姓名越來越多？) D2

(3) 今天最高温度是多少？最低温度是多少？

(4) 你今年最难忘的一天是哪天？(你今年最難忘的一天是哪天？)

C. Matching Exercise in Converting Written-style Chinese to Spoken-style Chinese

In the blank in front of each written-style Chinese expression in the left-hand column, write the letter of the corresponding spoken-style equivalent from the right-hand column.

____男	a) 一号(一號)
____一元	b) 男的
____一儿一女(一兒一女)	c) 一点(一點)
____一角	d) 女的
____一时(一時)	e) 的
____一日	f) 一块(一塊)
____之	g) 一毛
____女	h) 一个儿子、一个女儿 (一個兒子、一個女兒)

D. Translation from English into Written-style Chinese

Based on the written-style expressions in Exercise C, above, translate the following English expressions into written-style Chinese.

(1) fifty cents

(2) six o'clock

(3) three dollars

(4) one man and one woman

(5) the eighteenth of the month

(6) three sons and four daughters

Reading and Writing Exercises for Lesson 10-2

NAME ______________________ COURSE ______________________ DATE ______________________

A. Transcribe what you hear on the accompanying audio disc into Chinese characters.

(1)

(2)

(3)

B. If a reference is given after a question, answer based on the referenced part of the Reading Exercises. If no reference is indicated, you may answer any way you wish

(1) 王大海的女朋友为什么生气了？(王大海的女朋友為什麼生氣了？) A10

(2) 为什么要离老毛远一点儿？(為什麼要離老毛遠一點兒？) D2

(3) 你喜欢冷的天气吗？热的天气呢？(你喜歡冷的天氣嗎？熱的天氣呢？)

(4) 美国什么地方又干又热？(美國什麼地方又乾又熱？)

C. Sign

Read the following sign, which was posted outside a university canteen:

What do you think is the topic of the sign?

___

Transcribe the title of the sign into Pinyin.

___

Where do you think this sign is from, mainland China or Taiwan? Why?

___

What happens from 7:00 to 8:00?

___

What do you think probably takes place from 5:00 to 6:30?

___

What do you think takes place from 11:00 to 1:00?

___

Perhaps you can guess that the word 周末 (週末) **zhōumò** in the last line means "weekend." Knowing that, translate the last line of the sign into English:

___

Reading and Writing Exercises for Lesson 10-3

NAME ______________ COURSE ______________ DATE ______________

A. Transcribe what you hear on the accompanying audio disc into Chinese characters.

(1)

(2)

(3)

B. If a reference is given after a question, answer based on the referenced part of the Reading Exercises. If no reference is indicated, you may answer any way you wish.

(1) 别的人看得出来看不出来那个人六十岁了？(別的人看得出來看不出來那個人六十歲了？) A3

(2) 这几天台北是不是天天都下雨？(這幾天台北是不是天天都下雨？) B1

(3) 最近几天本地的天气怎么样？(最近幾天本地的天氣怎麼樣？)

(4) 你最近怎么样？(你最近怎麼樣？)

C. Radical Differentiation Exercise

In each group of four characters, there is one character that does not share the same radical as the other three. Circle it. Then, in the blank to the right, write the radical of the other three characters as well as the English meaning of that radical. (All characters in this exercise are in simplified script, but you should be able to do this exercise even if you're studying only traditional characters.)

件	街	行	很	________
学	字	店	定	________
住	往	何	低	________
字	安	写	定	________
你	他	们	忙	________
金	饭	钟	钱	________
家	定	买	实	________
海	没	津	准	________
轻	较	车	和	________
谢	谁	清	请	________
怎	忘	点	您	________
次	冷	河	准	________
忙	校	样	概	________
打	找	物	换	________
城	现	块	场	________
要	票	妹	姓	________
热	然	怎	点	________
店	原	广	度	________

Reading and Writing Exercises for Lesson 10-4

NAME ________________ COURSE ________________ DATE ________________

A. Transcribe what you hear on the accompanying audio disc into Chinese characters.

(1)

(2)

(3)

B. If a reference is given after a question, answer based on the referenced part of the Reading Exercises. If no reference is indicated, you may answer any way you wish.

(1) 万太太的儿子说现在美国年轻人都怎么样？(萬太太的兒子說現在美國年輕人都怎麼樣？) B2

(2) 高家的人为什么都很高兴？(高家的人為什麼都很高興？) D1

(3) 你刚来的时候，喜欢不喜欢本地的气候？(你剛來的時候，喜歡不喜歡本地的氣候？)

(4) 我已经吃过晚饭了，你呢？(我已經吃過晚飯了，你呢？)

C. Comparison with 比: Who's Taller Than Who?

(1) 小林比李太太高吗？(小林比李太太高嗎？)

(2) 小林比小王高吗？(小林比小王高嗎？)

(3) 小王比小林高吗？(小王比小林高嗎？)

(4) 小王比李太太高吗？(小王比李太太高嗎？)

(5) 李太太比小林高吗？(李太太比小林高嗎？)

(6) 李太太比小王高吗？(李太太比小王高嗎？)

(7) 这三个人里头，谁最高？(這三個人裡頭，誰最高？)

(8) 这三个人里头，谁第二高？(這三個人裡頭，誰第二高？)

Translation Exercises for *BMC Reading & Writing* Units A, B, and 1-10

Translation Exercises for Unit A

NAME ______________________ COURSE ______________________ DATE ______________________

Instructions: Translate the following into Chinese characters. If you have forgotten a word or character, check in the corresponding lesson of your textbook or consult the glossaries.

(1) Write the city and phone number: **Beijing 66913251**

(2) Write the city and phone number: **Taipei 2911-5183**

(3) Write the city and phone number: **Taishan 5619388**

(4) Write the city and phone number: **Taichung 2237-4156**

(5) Write this personal name (one possible way that you've learned): **Li Jing**

(6) Write this personal name (one possible way that you've learned): **Lin Taisheng**

(7) Write this personal name (one possible way that you've learned): **Wang Daming**

(8) Write this personal name (one possible way that you've learned): **He Jingsheng**

(9) Write this personal name (one possible way that you've learned): **Lin Mingshan**

(10) Write this personal name (one possible way that you've learned): **He Wenzhong**

Translation Exercises for Unit B

NAME ______________________ COURSE ______________________ DATE ______________________

Instructions: Translate the following into Chinese characters. If you have forgotten a word or character, check in the corresponding lesson of your textbook or consult the glossaries.

(1) Write the city and phone number: **Hong Kong 2696-5437**

(2) Write the city and phone number: **Shanghai 53594968**

(3) Write this personal name (one possible way that you've learned): **Jin Tianhu**

(4) Write this personal name (one possible way that you've learned): **Lin Anshan**

(5) Write the following address: **Tianjin Avenue**

(6) Write the following address: **Nanjing West Road**

(7) Write the following: **person from Taiwan**

(8) Write the following geographical name: **Henan Province**

(9) Write the following address (watch the order!): **Guangzhou City, Guangdong Province**

(10) Write the following address (watch the order!): **Chengdu City, Sichuan Province**

Translation Exercises for Unit 1

NAME ______________________ COURSE ______________________ DATE ______________________

Instructions: Translate the following into Chinese characters. If you have forgotten a word or character, check in the corresponding lesson of your textbook or consult the glossaries.

(1) Is Chinese hard?

(2) He is not too busy. And you?

(3) They (*male* and *female*) have all left.

(4) She is not too well. And Mrs. Wang?

(5) Mrs. Lin, Ms. Xie, thank you (*plural*)!

(6) I'm very busy; I'll be leaving first now.

(7) Little He, are you also going to Beijing?

(8) Old Gao, how are you? Please sit down, please sit down!

(9) We're all very well, thanks. And what about them (*female*)?

(10) They (*female*) are also all very well. How about you (*plural*)?

Translation Exercises for Unit 2

NAME ______________________ COURSE ______________ DATE ______________

Instructions: Translate the following into Chinese characters. If you have forgotten a word or character, check in the corresponding lesson of your textbook or consult the glossaries.

(1) Please don't call me "Little He." Thanks!

(2) This must be a Taiwanese person's name?

(3) Miss Li, I suppose you must be very happy.

(4) This is my old roommate; her name is Gao Jinjin.

(5) Excuse me, what country is your roommate from?

(6) A: Are all of you Chinese? B: None of us is Chinese.

(7) Which company is called “Sino-American Company”?

(8) A: Are all of you Americans? B: Not all of us are Americans.

(9) Mr. Wen didn’t bring name cards; Mrs. Lin didn’t bring name cards, either.

(10) A: What’s your honorable surname? B: My last name is Wang. My name is Wang Dongshan.

Translation Exercises for Unit 3

NAME ______________________ COURSE ______________ DATE ______________

Instructions: Translate the following into Chinese characters. If you have forgotten a word or character, check in the corresponding lesson of your textbook or consult the glossaries.

(1) I'm 18 years old this year.

(2) Your older sister is 21, right?

(3) In that case, let's take the 9:15 one.

(4) Two male teachers, two female teachers.

(5) She is going at 3:00. What time are you going?

(6) How old are you? (*the full form of the question*)

(7) A: How much is that one? B: $2,500. A: Too expensive!

(8) One half are male students, one half are female students.

(9) How many male teachers? How many female teachers? (*be polite!*)

(10) A: How many hours? B: About half an hour—no, an hour and a half!

Translation Exercises for Unit 4

NAME ______________________ COURSE ______________________ DATE ______________________

Instructions: Translate the following into Chinese characters. If you have forgotten a word or character, check in the corresponding lesson of your textbook or consult the glossaries.

(1) Who is she? What's her last name?

(2) Japanese is comparatively difficult, right?

(3) Mr. and Mrs. Wan have never been to America.

(4) Today is what month, what day? How about tomorrow?

(5) I don't have an older sister. Do you have an older sister?

(6) November 12th? November 12th is precisely my birthday!

(7) Fridays, Saturdays, and Sundays it's open; Mondays it's closed.

(8) This is my third time coming to China; I'm going to stay two weeks.

(9) When does that company open (*its doors*), and when does it close (*its doors*)?

(10) The population of Xian is relatively smaller, it seems it has only eight million people.

Translation Exercises for Unit 5

NAME ____________________ COURSE ____________________ DATE ____________________

Instructions: Translate the following into Chinese characters. If you have forgotten a word or character, check in the corresponding lesson of your textbook or consult the glossaries.

(1) This place's hotels are all too expensive.

(2) Excuse me, is there a person in this seat?

(3) She's learning Chinese at Beijing University.

(4) That thing which you are looking for is over there.

(5) Do you know where it would be relatively better to eat?

(6) Old Li is a laborer; however, Little Li is a college student.

(7) Our colleague is going to return to her native country in July.

(8) I want that Pentium that is on top. Where is the on-off switch?

(9) If you're looking for a student but he/she is not there, you can also ask the teacher.

(10) I searched on top, searched on the bottom, searched inside, searched outside, searched left, and searched right, but in all cases it wasn't there.

Translation Exercises for Unit 6

NAME ______________________ COURSE ______________________ DATE ______________________

Instructions: Translate the following into Chinese characters. If you have forgotten a word or character, check in the corresponding lesson of your textbook or consult the glossaries.

(1) She really likes her boyfriend.

(2) You're 50? You look very young!

(3) They work at China Northwest Company.

(4) Where were you born and where did you grow up?

(5) The food here is delicious! I like to eat it very much.

(6) What grade in elementary school is your daughter in?

(7) The principal of Taipei American School is my good friend.

(8) My last name is Lin; I forgot to give you (*polite!*) my name card.

(9) A: Why doesn't she work? B: Because her son is still small, she can't work.

(10) In our family there are eight people. I have one older brother, two older sisters, and two younger sisters. I don't have younger brothers.

Translation Exercises for Unit 7

NAME ______________________ COURSE ______________________ DATE ______________________

Instructions: Translate the following into Chinese characters. If you have forgotten a word or character, check in the corresponding lesson of your textbook or consult the glossaries.

(1) I've heard that you're from Shanghai. When did you arrive?

(2) She originally worked in a factory; now she's a college student.

(3) I feel that after you arrive in China, you can learn many things.

(4) Did you go alone to the Great Wall? Did you go together with a friend?

(5) In the beginning I didn't much like Japanese, but now I like it very much.

(6) I've learned about 200 Chinese characters; some I can write, others I can't write.

(7) My cousin (*younger*, *female*) doesn't live in Taichung City, she lives in Taichung County.

(8) Taiwanese, at first I learned it in the U.S. Later I again studied in Taiwan for several months.

(9) I can speak spoken Chinese, and I can also write Chinese characters, but I don't write them very well.

(10) Five years ago I learned Cantonese, but now I have forgotten all of it. (*don't use 都 for "all"; use what you learned in this lesson*)

Translation Exercises for Unit 8

NAME ______________________ COURSE ______________ DATE ______________

Instructions: Translate the following into Chinese characters. If you have forgotten a word or character, check in the corresponding lesson of your textbook or consult the glossaries.

(1) Excuse me, how do you get to Tiananmen?

(2) She is probably waiting for me at Capital Airport.

(3) Please walk toward the south; don't walk toward the north.

(4) Old Sister, how many pieces of luggage do you want to bring?

(5) I have heard that one person can only take one piece of luggage.

(6) That place is very close to here; why do you say it's far from here?

(7) If you go by car, how long a time is needed to go from Beijing to Tianjin?

(8) A: Who is the driver? B: Mr. Xie. I called him on the telephone an hour ago.

(9) On this road there are too many cars; we have no choice but to change to another road.

(10) Because there are too many cars, at the time when people get off from work, traffic is not very good.

Translation Exercises for Unit 9

NAME ______________________ COURSE ______________________ DATE ______________________

Instructions: Translate the following into Chinese characters. If you have forgotten a word or character, check in the corresponding lesson of your textbook or consult the glossaries.

(1) Who knows how many animals the Beijing Zoo has?

(2) Do you sell bus tickets here? I need to buy two tickets.

(3) Remember to eat breakfast at 7:00 tomorrow morning.

(4) I just arrived at Capital Airport; there are too many people there!

(5) I can't find that Chinese language center that you talked about.

(6) First find the public bus station, then get on the bus and buy tickets.

(7) The next station is none other than Zoo; you should prepare to get off.

(8) From here please go straight to the intersection; in about 3 minutes you'll arrive.

(9) She's not a local person, she's Japanese; therefore, she's not very clear either where the Peace Hotel is.

(10) Formerly, street car tickets only cost ten cents; later they cost fifty cents; I hear that now they cost a dollar.

Translation Exercises for Unit 10

NAME ____________________ COURSE ____________________ DATE ____________________

Instructions: Translate the following into Chinese characters. If you have forgotten a word or character, check in the corresponding lesson of your textbook or consult the glossaries.

(1) The weather here is both dry and hot, and it seldom rains.

(2) Starting from this evening, it's likely to get colder and colder.

(3) Your spoken Vietnamese, you already speak it very accurately.

(4) That classmate of yours seems (to have the appearance of being) very sad.

(5) What is the high temperature tomorrow? And what is the low temperature?

(6) Actually, it's possible you can't see from looking, but it's just drizzling right now.

(7) You came at just the right time; the weather today is too good, neither cold nor hot.

(8) Recently it's been so hot one could die; in the future, I don't necessarily want to live in this place.

(9) A: Good morning! Come in. B: The weather today is not bad; the sun has come out!

(10) I feel that the climate on the east coast is better than the west coast, but my roommate feels that the climate on the east coast is not as good as on the west coast. (*don't use* 可是*; instead, use a synonym of* 可是 *that you learned in this unit*)